CHRI in Atlantic Canada

~~~~~~~~~~

STORIES True *AND* False, Past *AND* Present

DAVID GOSS

Foreword by GERRY BOWLER
author of Santa Claus, A Biography

NIMBUS
PUBLISHING
—— NIMBUS.CA ——

Nimbus Publishing Limited
3660 Strawberry Hill Street, Halifax, NS, B3K 5A9
(902) 455-4286 nimbus.ca

Printed and bound in Canada

NB1382

Cover design: Heather Bryan
Interior design: Jenn Embree
Editor: Emily MacKinnon

Library and Archives Canada Cataloguing in Publication

Goss, David, author
Christmas in Atlantic Canada : stories true and false, past
and present / David Goss ; foreword by Gerry Bowler.
Includes bibliographical references.
Issued in print and electronic formats.
ISBN 978-1-77108-687-5 (softcover).—ISBN 978-1-77108-688-2 (HTML)

1. Christmas—Atlantic Provinces—History. 2. Christmas—Atlantic Provinces—
Anecdotes. I. Bowler, G. Q., 1948-, writer of foreword II. Title.

GT4987.15.G67 2018   394.266309715   C2018-902879-3
                                                           C2018-902880-7

Nimbus Publishing acknowledges the financial support for its publishing activities from the Government of Canada, the Canada Council for the Arts, and from the Province of Nova Scotia. We are pleased to work in partnership with the Province of Nova Scotia to develop and promote our creative industries for the benefit of all Nova Scotians.

ᏉDEDICATION

━⟨ᴑᴑᴑᴑᴑ⟩━

This book is the result of the efforts my mother, Marion Aileen Chetley, and my father, Abram Young Goss, made to ensure my earliest Christmases were such a delight that it led to a lifelong love for, and fascination with, the season. This was further developed when Donna Marie (Whitaker) and I married in 1966; we had two children, Derek Wayne and Christy Dawn (Bigney), to share the December festivities with through crafting, storytelling, carol singing, and festive meals, which we still do to this day. I am grateful to them all for everything they have done and continue to do. I dedicate this book to them.

CONTENTS

⟨O⟩FOREWORD

⟿⟩⟩⟩⟩⟨⟵

⟨O⟩hristmas is just about the biggest thing there is. It is the world's favourite festival with over a billion participants spending a twelfth of their year under its sway. It is an engine of the global economy, as well as a time for spiritual reflection on a baby in a Bethlehem stable two millennia ago. We spend weeks preparing for its arrival: baking, brewing, shopping, wrapping, cleaning, rehearsing, travelling, meditating, fasting, decorating, and hoping. We mark its arrival by eating and drinking, singing and dancing, visiting and hosting, and when it is all over and we are exhausted and worrying about how we will pay for all the excess, we know we will happily do it all again next year.

Around the world Christmas makes people eagerly do things they would not ordinarily do: like bringing dead trees into Canadian living rooms and decorating them with ornaments that have been hidden away for the last eleven months; like marching with your Mexican neighbours through the streets for nine consecutive nights, pretending to be the holy family seeking lodging; like getting turkeys drunk in Portugal; keeping carp in the bathtub in Hungary; or leaving out treats for birds in Sweden.

At what other time of the year will you see children beating pooping logs, families putting candles in ice blocks on graves, shaggy figures sweeping the streets clean of demons, or neighbours singing in the snow outside your door?

The festive season is toasted with cava in Spain, bowls of wassail in England, *cola de mono* in Chile, eggnog in America, cold beer on the beach in Australia, and Atholl Brose in Scotland. Christmas is the time of year for special foods: eels in Italy, pudding in Wales, Kentucky Fried Chicken in Japan, tourtière in Québec, *pan dulce* in Argentina, the black fast in Ireland, and the famous twelve desserts of southern France. Nor are the dead forgotten—in many cultures, a place is set and food is left out for the spirits of the family members who have passed on, but who are believed to return home on Christmas Eve.

No other time of the year offers such wonderful music, from the majestic *Messiah* by George Frideric Handel to the light-hearted "Santa Claus is Comin' to Town" by J. Fred Coots and Haven Gillespie. We sing songs that are centuries old like "Of the Father's Love Begotten," based on a poem written by the bodyguard of a Roman emperor when Christianity was just beginning. Another, a medieval melody, was written by a sorrowing monk who dreamed that angels came to comfort him; the angels took him by the hand and led him in a dance while one sang "In Dulci Jubilo." When he woke, he wrote the music in the form of a carol that became "Good Christian Men Rejoice." We sing of three kings of the Orient, King Wenceslas of Bohemia, little Suzy Snowflake, snowmen with top hats, reindeer with luminous noses, holly, ivy, roses of such virtue, and a baby in a makeshift cradle.

Any child reading this will wonder why I have taken so long getting to the important part of the holiday: the presents and the magical gift-bringer who will deliver them on Christmas Eve, or New Year's Eve, or Twelfth Night, depending on location and tradition. One automatically thinks of Santa Claus in this regard but, though he is culturally dominant, he was not the first of these nocturnal figures. Around the world little ones will also be pinning their hopes on St. Nicholas, Grandfather Frost, Joulupukki, the Yule Lads, or *los Reyes Magos*. Lest you think this gift-bringing role belongs only to men, consider Tante Arie of France, Befana of Italy, or Mother Goody of eastern Canada. When you think of Santa's helpers, you must not forget Zwarte Piet (Black Peter), Black Piet (or Krampus) who travels with *das Christkindl*. We are well acquainted in Canada with the reindeer who pull Santa's sleigh, but children around the world know that the Gift-Bringer also relies on six white kangaroos, camels, mules, or a team of alligators led by a red-nosed werewolf.

Though Christmas unites us globally in many ways of sacred and secular celebration, it is also a time when we choose to announce our particular, smaller-scale loyalties: we mark the season in the ways our family, locality, or religion has always done with the food we eat, the songs we sing, and the customs we practice. We value Christmas tradition over innovation. It is here that folklorists and chroniclers of specific areas become so important, noting the regional differences, the ways in which myriads of communities distinguish themselves from each other in the manners of the season.

David Goss is one of Canada's most distinguished regional historians, well versed in the past of the Atlantic provinces and particularly knowledgeable in the ways Christmas has been celebrated along our coast. In this book you will come to appreciate that the area has many unique features that have drawn on the customs of the various peoples who have settled the land—the French, English, Irish, Scots, Germans, and Americans— to create a Christmas that is like nowhere else. You will learn about the New Year's Baby and Queen Mab; about mummering and Belsnickling; and about rappie pie, chicken bones, and barley toys. You'll read about Christmases that were almost cancelled, and the Order of Good Cheer. You are certain to come away from these pages entertained, educated, and a bigger fan of Christmas.

Gerry Bowler, author of *The World Encyclopedia of Christmas; Santa Claus: A Biography; Christmas in the Crosshairs*, and editor of *The World's Greatest Christmas Stories*.
Winnipeg, Manitoba
Palm Sunday 2018

AUTHOR'S NOTE

When I was in grade four, back in 1954, Miss Blackie, who became Mrs. Howe that year, told me I should write a book. She told me if I were to be successful, the book had to be about something I was crazy about. At that time, the last horses were on the streets of Saint John, and they fascinated me. I chose to do a book about the noble creatures. Mrs. Howe sparked something that year and it has resulted in some four thousand published articles, eighteen books, and a Walk 'n' Talk series that shares stories of my home city every Tuesday in summer (which has just finished its forty-first season). Mrs. Howe's advice to choose something you're crazy about when writing was bang on, and that is how this book came to be. Looking back, I find that about 25 percent of all the magazine articles and newspaper pieces I've written have been about Christmas. One of the eighteen books was also about Christmas, but only about how it was celebrated in New Brunswick, and since it came out in 1997, I have worked to expand that knowledge to include details from all across Canada, with a particular focus on the portion of the region I know best, Atlantic Canada.

Will you find answers to all your questions about Christmas in this area? No, because there is such a body of information to encapsulate that it would have taken a much larger book than the one you are holding. Many things were also part of family celebrations and not documented in the newspapers, diaries, books, magazines, and personal interviews that are the basis for this content. But there is so much here that was fascinating and new to this researcher that I am sure it will bring the same pleasure to you to learn about how our Christmas came to be.

Merry Christmas!

CHRISTMAS as it DEVELOPED on the EASTERN SEABOARD

﹏᷾᷾᷾᷾﹏

The marking of old-time Christmas has become widely popular during the holiday season, which itself has been developing and changing worldwide since given official status by Pope Liberius in 354.

What is now considered an "old-fashioned Christmas" often includes customs that developed—or were revived and reworked—after Christmas had been cancelled in 1647 in England. The Puritans had come into power after beheading Charles the First and decided Christmas had become a massive drunken time. This situation lasted until 1660, when Christmas was restored by an act of Parliament. In this time, some of the celebratory elements were lost, but when revived, those ideas that were remembered of the pre-cancellation era came to America with the German and English settlers and spread along the eastern seaboard. From there, the ideas moved both east and west with the settlement of both Canada and the United States. The redevelopment of Christmas reached its zenith in the early to middle nineteenth century, especially during the Victorian era. This also happened to be when what became Atlantic Canada's primary trading partner was England. Thus, settlers brought their ways of celebrating, and merchants filled their stores with goods, magazines, and books from overseas. This all affected the ways Christmas became the celebration it is today, and this influence and development is the focus of the chapters that follow.

To understand this more fully, it is helpful to give some background on various elements of Christmas as they developed outside Atlantic Canada, and then focus on how they came to and were marked in each of the four provinces.

The beginning was long before the first explorers came to North and South America and brought European ideas of celebrating the season with them. If they happened to be on this side of the Atlantic on the twenty-fifth of December, accounts exist of them making references to marking the day.

Winnipeg author Gerry Bowler's *The World Encyclopedia of Christmas* records such observances. Under the headline "December 25th events," he notes a Mass held by Magellan off the Brazilian coast in 1519, a celebration in 1535 with Jacques Cartier at Stadacona (Quebec), and followed three years later by the first Catholic Mass in Mexico celebrated by Fray Pedro de Gante.

In 1604, Bowler notes, "The French settlers on islands off Maine observed the first American Christmas." In this he is referring to St. Croix Island on the New Brunswick border between Canada and the United States and the expedition of Pierre Dugua de Mons and Samuel de Champlain. This was the first attempt at overwintering north of Florida and it was not a success; over half of the party's seventy-nine men died. However, though no document exists to prove it, some historians believe they would have celebrated Christmas with traditional religious services as they had religious leaders among their party.

Among these is writer G. J. Gillespie, who explored the notion of this first Christmas celebration in the December 1956 issue of *Atlantic Advocate*, where he stated: "There is nothing in the written chronicles to tell how the adventurers from beyond the wide sea spent that first Christmas in the land of Acadia." However, he then continued his thoughts by saying

Champlain later founded the "Order of Good Cheer" across the Bay of Fundy in Nova Scotia, and recorded celebrations of Christmas in Quebec as the decade ended. He concluded: "The characters of the courtly Champlain and Sieur de Mons [Pierre Dugua] are evidence enough that the occasion must have been marked by what festivities their limited resources afforded."

Thus, Bowler's encyclopedia designates the St. Croix experience as the first American Christmas, while others say it was the first "white Christmas" in order to get around an earlier observation that was recorded in older settlements in Florida.

And what of the period between that 1604 event and those between 1850 and 1900, when most scholars—Bowler included—say the season really became what we know today as an old-fashioned Christmas?

There is plenty of material to be found in Bowler's *World Encyclopedia of Christmas* and in other books, documents, and papers. In Bowler's work, we find such events as John Smith in Jamestown boasting of "finer food and more warmth in Virginia than at home in England" in 1608; Huron converts performing a Christmas play at Michilimackinac in 1678; Christmas hymns sung for the first time in Boston's Old North church in 1759, all of which could be part of the drama of old-time Christmas celebration today.

At this time, on the British North American side of the border, most accounts of Christmas come from the records of the fur traders or the Jesuit Relations. They observed December twenty-fifth as Christmas, noted that prayers were offered and some attempt at feasting was made, and that all felt a longing for the comforts of the celebration in homes far across the sea.

Another important aspect of the holiday season, of course, is music, and it is believed that it was in 1642 that the only Canadian carol to become known internationally was composed. The haunting "Jesus Ahatonhia," or "Jesus is Born," that begins, "'Twas in the moon of wintertime..." It was Père Jean de Brébeuf's attempt at explaining the birth of Christ to the Hurons.

The Maritime provinces were collectively known as "Acadia" during this period and were being battled over by two adversaries: Charles de Menou d'Aulnay and Charles La Tour. Yet, in 1644, according to writer Doug MacLellan, they took time to engage in "laughter, dancing, and merrymaking," on Christmas Day, after being led in the "Notre Pere," or "Lord's Prayer," by La Tour himself.

Loyalist Christmas 1783, as depicted by artist E. J. Russell.

However, following that, there was a great period of silence. The earliest known letter sent from the Saint John area, written by James Simonds, who settled at the mouth of the River St. John from Newburyport, Massachusetts, does not mention Christmas at all, even though it was written on December 26, 1764.

It is not until 1783, when British Loyalists settled in the Maritime provinces following the American Revolution, that we have any further record of Christmas in Atlantic Canada. Those who came later to what would eventually become Canada were used to comfortable, even lavish, Christmases similar to the ones Philip Fithian wrote of in 1773 from Virginia, saying, "Nothing is now to be heard of in conversation but the balls, fox-hunts, the fine entertainments, and the good fellowship, which are exhibited at the approaching Christmas." But such Christmases were a quarter-century in the future when the Loyalists arrived. Pressed by simple survival, it was years before comments about Christmas were made in diaries or journals. Even then they were simple statements like, "A most excellent Christmas, warm enough for pleasure," without any detail as to what made it "excellent," or what "pleasure" might have been undertaken, as is the case with the Reverend Dibblee's diary of 1806–1822.

Influenced by British traditions, Christmas celebrations in Atlantic Canada began to flourish in the early 1800s. This was especially true in the capital cities of Fredericton, Halifax, and St. John's. In Fredericton and Halifax, the regularly changing British Regiments were acquainted with the latest ideas of the season from overseas, and were homesick for the kind of Christmas that would have been celebrated in England. Their ideas became entrenched. In St. John's, considered by the British as a seasonal fishing ground rather than a colony until the 1800s, most inhabitants left during the winter months. However, that started to change as the nineteenth century began, and the population grew from 3,000 to 10,000 by 1815. Most settlers were English and Irish, and they brought Christmas customs like hunting the wren and burning the Yule log, which are just memories now, but also mummering, which is still a distinctive element of Newfoundland Christmas to this day. The military presence was most important to the colony, as building fortifications created work, and the workmen and the military men patronized local merchants and drinking and eating establishments. As well, military dances would have been held throughout the year, and especially at Christmas and New Years, and this meant interaction and exchange of ideas between the sailors, soldiers, and those who were permanent residents.

An account of Christmas in Halifax, written by Sir John Wentworth to his friend Colonel Edward Winslow in 1785, spoke of an Assembly Ball to mark the New Year, and that his wife, Frances Deering, who had been born in Boston and lived in New Hampshire before coming to Nova Scotia, so enjoyed "shak(ing) her shoes," on the dance floor that she became known as the "married belle of Halifax."

In 1804, Lady Jane Hunter, wife of the Commander-in-Chief of his Majesty's Forces in North America, visited her husband in the colonies, and while there, wrote letters home that gave a detailed description of Christmas as it was marked at the garrison in Fredericton. She wrote of the "gay" season just before Christmas, and of everybody "flying about in sleighs in the morning and going to 'gregorys' [she referred to these as 'stupid card-parties'] and dances in the evenings." She also wrote of "Queen Mab," a "great favorite of the little folks in this and the other provinces,

Barracks in Fredericton, 1834 (Provincial Archives of New Brunswick P37/345).

and if they hang up their stocking on Christmas Eve she always pops something good into it."

Ideas were also coming over the border from the United States, as those clear of the Puritan influence—which kept Christmas from being widely celebrated in the Boston area until the 1870s—were also embracing the season.

While what follows can't be taken to be the norm, it was the experience of John Fairfield, Governor of the State of Maine, whose account of "Christmas in Augusta" in 1840 is part of a larger collection of his letters written from 1836 to 1847. He described the holiday thusly: "Yesterday, I attended religious services at the Church. The house was very prettily decorated and the service appropriate." Later, Fairfield attended a "fine Christmas party" given by Mrs. Dan'l Williams, where he enjoyed "an abundance of 'creature comforts' and also had a fine treat in the singing of some old-fashioned tunes, such as 'Shelburne.' In this example, we can see the emergence of Christmas traditions that have become associated with what we could call an old-time Christmas.

And the process was about to speed up; festivities enjoyed by socialites were to become more common during the second half of the nineteenth century. It was at this time in New York City that two events occurred that were to have long-lasting effects on the celebration of the season. The first was the publication of Washington Irving's bestseller, *Knickerbocker's History of New York* (1809), in which he urged Americans to begin marking Christmas in the more robust way the English did. The second had an even greater influence, though initially it was not clergyman Clement Clarke Moore's intent to do anything more than entertain his own family at Christmas in 1822. His poem marked the beginning of the veneration of Santa Claus, which grew out of ideas in Irving's prose, and from the Dutch settler's lore about the visit of St. Nicholas on the sixth of December. Moore took these ideas and wrote what has come to be called the most famed twenty-eight couplets in the English language, "A Visit from St. Nicholas," known now by its first line, "'Twas the night before Christmas."

To show how quickly it spread, we need only look across the border to New Brunswick, where a handwritten copy of the famed poem on paper watermarked 1825, with text signed "CCM" is held in the New Brunswick Museum along with other letters from Moore to the Odell family. The letter is believed to have been sent to Jonathan Odell (though by then he was dead) as he had been Moore's godfather and kept in touch with the family.

Five years later, on December 25, 1830, the poem appeared in the *New Brunswick Courier*, with Blixen, not Blitzen, as one of the eight reindeer Moore had named. That was its first appearance in Atlantic Canada, thus acquainting New Brunswick children with a new gift giver to replace Queen Mab, but not a new way of receiving gifts, for she too had used the stocking as a gift depository.

The next idea to come along and gain universal appeal was the Christmas tree. When the first public tree was displayed is a matter of much debate in both Canada and the United States.

During the Revolutionary War in the United States, the Hessians, of German background, brought what is said to be Martin Luther's idea of a lit tree to the battlefield. Some half a century later, in 1832, it was Bostonian Charles Follen, also of German descent, who is said to have been the first to decorate a tree in his home. However, there are many other claims to being first, but Follen's tree was publicized in Sunday School papers of the time so this moved the idea along more so than any other of the claims to being first. A description written by Harriet Martineau at the time that predicted the "Christmas tree will become one of the most flourished exotic's of New

Bachelor's Christmas, from the Daily Telegraph, *December 24, 1892.*

England," has certainly come true.

In Canada, the first Christmas tree appeared in Sorel, Quebec, in 1781. This was approximately the time of the first tree on American battlefields, and again, it's German-born Friedrich von Riedesel who does the introduction. Sometimes Halifax is given credit for being home of the first tree, but in reality, it was many years later in 1846 when William Pryor erected and decorated a tree with glass balls (imported from Germany for his German wife).

In 1848, an engraving in the *Illustrated London News* of Queen Victoria, her German husband, Albert, and their children enjoying their Christmas tree in Windsor Castle circulated widely in North America at this time, thus increasing interest in the idea of families doing the same. However, it was slow in development. One early description written in 1863 by fifty-four-year old John E. Godfrey describing a Christmas in Bangor, Maine, said: "The last week was Christmas week and more devoted to the people to pleasure than business. A great change has taken place in this respect since I was a boy. Christmas was very little thought of then, Christmas presents were rarely given." Then after discussing some gifts he had received, he concluded his note with comment on the newest development in Bangor: "The first parish people...had a Christmas tree; a great innovation on orthodox notions..." and "the Unitarians had a Christmas tree at City Hall."

The earliest photograph of Santa discovered during research for this book is this image taken by Saint John photographer G. F. Simonson, who was in business on Charlotte Street between 1874 and 1875.

In 1851, Mark Carr, a Catskill farmer, brought trees to the streets of New York to sell, thus showing the idea took off more rapidly in the big cities. In Canada's Atlantic provinces, a tree in a store window in the 1880s would be sufficient enough to draw a large crowd. However, trees in the home were still not common until about 1900.

An Episcopal church in New York City was the first to have a Christmas tree in their Sunday school in 1847. It was the 1880s before trees became a part of the tradition in most Atlantic Sunday schools, and if it was combined with a visit from Santa, it was always after the twenty-fifth, never before, to respect the sacredness of Christmas Day.

Illustrations of Santa Claus by Sherman and Smith started appearing in *New York City Magazine* in 1843, according to James H. Barnett's 1954 book *The American Christmas*. Karal Ann Marling notes Theodore C. Boyd created a depiction of Santa in an 1848 gift book for children in her 2000 book, *Merry Christmas*. Both Barnett and Marling agree it was Thomas Nast's depictions of Santa on the cover of *Harper's Weekly* from 1863 to the mid-1880s that formed most youngsters' idea of what Santa looked like, unless they lived in a large city centre. Marling notes that Philadelphia stores had started to put Kris Kringles in their windows beginning in the 1840s, and Boston followed in the 1870s.

Leigh Eric Schmidt's *Consumer Rites: The Buying and Selling of American Holidays* adds to Marling's information, saying it was Philadelphia confectioner and caterer James Parkinson who claimed to be the first to use the image of Kris Kringle for merchandising in 1841. This would have been a depiction, not a live costumed Santa.

In New Brunswick, children saw their first live Santa as played by Fredericton confectioner Charles A. Sampson in December 1872. Earlier that month he had advertised that he would arrange for Santa to deliver gifts to all children whose parents placed orders from his stock, and indeed did so on Christmas Eve for four consecutive years. In addition, he opened his store on Christmas Day and distributed his leftover stock to the poor children of the city and surrounding area.

Once Sampson stopped his role of Santa, it wasn't until 1887 that Santa made another appearance in New Brunswick. Manchester Robertson Allison Limited, a dry goods and department store, brought their first costumed Santa to their Saint John department store. His appearance drew so many customers to the store window on the Saturday night before

Christmas that the *Globe* reported the whole street was blocked, two ladies fainted, and when the crowds refused to leave, managers had to drop the store's blinds. After that, Santa appeared daily for an hour at 9:30 A.M. and 8 P.M. and welcomed children to visit inside the store.

In *Merry Christmas*, Karal Ann Marling notes the first store with a costumed Santa in America was arranged by James Edgar, owner of the Boston Store in Brockton, Massachusetts, in 1890, three years after the success of the New Brunswick Santa. Though Christmas celebrations slowed following the American Revolution when New Englanders settled in Canada, Canadians not only caught up but surpassed their neighbours to the south in Christmas celebrations in some ways.

The TREE and GREENING

༺ⓞⓞⓞⓞ༻

No one can say for certain when evergreens became associated with Christmas, and when the first tree became such a universal part of the celebration. There are, for sure, a good many suppositions on the matter. The use of greens goes back to what are often called "pagan times," which is the era before the birth of Jesus Christ. For centuries people had brought evergreen boughs into their homes at the winter solstice, believing they were everlasting in nature and would bring back the sun. Ancient Romans also decorated their homes with greens, and nailed laurel over their doorways during the January Kalends, and gave each other gifts of green branches as symbols of good luck. When the Christian era began, and Pope Gregory in 325 declared December 25 to be the day of Christ's birth, the pagan and Roman symbolism gradually transferred to Christmas.

A great many legends about greenery sprouted from the manger story of Jesus's birth and the miracles of some of the early saints. They make great stories, but they are just that; there is no proof, only supposition.

The story of how St. Boniface (680–754) replaced the Druids' pagan oak with an evergreen is one of these tree-origin tales, and became better known during the Victorian era through retelling in Henry Van Dyke's *The Other Wise Man.*

Similarly, there is a story of Martin Luther (1483–1546) walking through the forest and seeing the stars dancing in the boughs of the evergreens. When he arrived home with a tree, he lit its branches up with candles. In *The World Encyclopedia of Christmas*, author Gerry Bowler dismisses this as "extremely unlikely." Even more strongly in a letter to your author, Bowler wrote: "Luther had nothing to do with the custom despite many websites that tell the tale."

Another story involves a hungry child wandering through the forest in Germany who was comforted in a forester's home. He was given supper, and the forester's child gave up his bed for the child, who it turned out, was the Christ Child. In the morning, he broke off a fir branch, planted it in the ground, and promised them the tree would always be green, would always bear fruit, and they would never be hungry. Touching, but not verifiable.

What is for sure, though, is that the Germans were the first to bring the tree into the home, and decorate it at Christmas, probably as early as the sixteenth century. The idea passed on to Britain when members of the Royal family, who had emigrated from Germany, brought the custom to London. Published images of their celebrations around the tree spread the idea through the world.

In Atlantic Canada there was one resident ahead of the Royal family: in 1846, Halifax merchant William Pryor set up a tree with glass ornaments in Coburg Cottage to please his German-born wife, Barbara.

As noted previously, an even earlier incident was in 1781 in Sorel, Quebec, where Baron Friedrich von Riedesel, commander of the Hessian (German) troops fighting on Britain's behalf in the American Revolution, set up a fir from the nearby forest and decorated it with white candles, as was the custom at the time in Germany. There is, of course, a period of thirty-five years between these two dates noted above. While no other claims have come forward to be annotated, it does not mean that at some time and place there was not someone who copied the Quebec tree and lighting. The same can be said for the period following the Halifax tree; it is very likely there were other early trees that simply were not recorded, but only enjoyed by families throughout the region.

It is in the 1880s that reports of greenery and decorated trees begin to show up with some regularity in the newspapers of the Atlantic region. Here are a few that reflect the range of places where such adornments were found:

Markets

The *Charlottetown Patriot*—December 22, 1893: "The Christmas Market today…was abundantly supplied…and the tables groaned under the immense supply of poultry and dairy products…and the venue was quite Xmas like with evergreens and other indications of the festive season."

Orphanages

The *Saint John Globe*—December 31, 1885: "A handsome tree, ablaze with lights and bearing precious fruit and toys and useful articles greeted the children of the Protestant Orphan's Home last evening. The children enjoyed a program of music."

Restaurants

The St. John's *Evening Telegram*—December 24, 1886: "The Queen restaurant (opposite) has been decorated with green boughs and Christmas trees, illuminated with vari-colored lamps between. Mr. Tupper shows quite a large stock of Christmas delicacies, and they are all good to eat."

Kindergartens

The *Halifax Evening Herald*—December 20, 1881: "The Christmas festival at the Froebel kindergarten…No. 41 Victoria Road took place yesterday. At the close of the exercises the Christmas tree was relieved of its burden and each pupil was the recipient of a present."

Fredericton Officer's Square Barracks

This military area is known to have been decorated with greens as early as 1808, based on information from a letter Lady Hunter posted to her family in England. In December of 1884, a writer for the *Fredericton Capital*, commenting on the effective use of greens in that year's decorating effort, noted, "It was difficult for one to believe that the work had been performed without the assistance of the gentler sex."

Churches

Long before commercial or home decorating became common, the churches, especially those of the Anglican body, decorated lavishly using greens and motto cards, but seldom trees, as for many the tree still had a pagan association. In Halifax in 1885, St. George's was described in the *Morning Chronicle* as having a chancel "wreathed with evergreen," and there was a "very effective holly cross on which red berries shone conspicuously." The holly, of course, was imported, and tribute was paid to F. W. Symonds, who arranged and paid for this annually. In Moncton, almost a decade earlier in 1877, a report in the *Times* described the Roman Catholic Chapel as "neatly decorated for Christmas," with motto board in white with gold letters with scriptural mottos, and "immediately above [these] were festoons of evergreen and the pillars were decorated with the same." This shows that Anglicans were not the only denomination adorning their churches with greenery. An entry from Newfoundland's *Evening Telegram* dated January 7, 1889, shows that the decorative effort sometimes extended beyond the church itself, and into the schoolroom. It stated, "The evergreens, ferns, dog berries, rose buds and tissue paper of various colors were so blended and artistically interwoven...the Chinese lanterns were displayed with such good taste...the scene was one of enchantment...our friends were almost inclined to believe themselves transported to fairyland."

The various papers consulted from Prince Edward Island did not provide much in the way of descriptions of greening in the churches. The various editors were content to comment on the times of services prior to Christmas Day, and on the attendance and music. In Summerside in 1880, the *Journal* reported that the Catholic Church was "crowded to over-flowing," and was contrasted with the Episcopal and Methodist churches,

20 ✷ DAVID GOSS

> T**n**is
> is,
> you
> see, a
> Christ-
> mas tree,
> one of the
> best type, too!
> and while, dear
> sir, 'tis not a
> fir, yet it was
> made "fir" you. 'Tis
> true, you see upon
> this tree no presents
> rich and rare; yet
> please be kind, and
> bear in mind, in wish
> the gifts are there. We now
> wish all, the short and tall,
> young, middle-aged and grey,
> the
> poor,
> the rich,
> white,
> black
> as pitch,
> •'A Merry Christmas" Day.

This is an example of the typesetter's art designed to catch the eye, with the words forming the image of a Christmas tree.

where the attendance in "both churches was small." Comments on the music were common, too, such as in 1894 at St. Dunstan's Cathedral, where it was stated in the *Daily Examiner* that Mozart's "Dona Nobis Pacem" was sung as the closing music of the service, which had been " a happy one." Other than saying "the sanctuary was tastefully decorated," there is no clue as to what this decorative effort looked like at this church.

All these public displays of greenery and trees led to more and more people taking on the idea of erecting a tree in the home. There is no printed record that can be consulted to illustrate exact percentages, but anecdotal evidence indicates the numbers were increasing.

In December 1890, the *Morning Chronicle*, in reaction to the growing numbers putting up a tree, published a column titled "The Christmas Tree: Things to consider in selecting and dressing it." It read: "A Christmas tree ought to be selected with special reference to the space it is to occupy, one with branches firm, not too broad, and quite tall is best. [...] The upper branches should be decorated before the tree is set up [by tying] white cotton batten, snowballs, and short loops," to the tips of the branches. Once the tree is in its stand, the article continued, "It is a good plan to hang gifts so that bright contrasting colors may set off the tree. Never use brown paper." As for those gaps in the branches, "dolls, bright-covered books, gaily painted toys, bright silk handkerchiefs, white scarves" could be used.

The final step was the addition of "liberal quantities of frost powder and a dozen or more packages of gilt," so that "under brilliant light, the tree can become a veritable creation of fairyland."

One study done across America—referred to in *The Christmas Tree Book* by Phillip V. Snyder—came to the conclusion that only one home in five had a tree before 1900. However, this changed rapidly in the opening years of the twentieth century, and the same study indicated that by the end the First World War, 80 percent of homes had a decorated tree. There is no reason to doubt this was also the case in Atlantic Canada. The availability of German-made ornaments at very reasonable prices in Woolworth's five-and-dime stores certainly helped in increasing the popularity of decorating an indoor tree.

There are many oral accounts that have been collected by museum staff in all four provinces from people who have shared similar stories of the early use of Christmas trees in their homes. Some folks recounted how the tree was not decorated until Christmas Eve, when the family would be called into the parlour to watch in wonder as candles fastened to the branches were lit. This seems like a bit of a tease, as it would be Christmas Day when the gifts would be distributed. Some remembered how there would be family members standing nearby with pails of sand and water in case the flames ignited the tree's branches. Others recalled that there would be no tree in the home on Christmas Eve, but they would hang their stocking over the fireplace, the expectation being Santa would fill them and also bring and decorate the tree. Sure enough, when they arose on the twenty-fifth, the tree would have been placed in the parlour and all the gifts from Santa would be arranged underneath, as if by magic. Whether this happened on the twenty-fourth or twenty-fifth, the common element of these stories is that the tree did not stay up very long—only a day or two in most homes.

⤙⟨⟨⟨⟨⟩⤚

The coming of the electric age—at least in the cities—led to the erection of brightly lit outdoor trees in town squares and parks and on some public buildings. One of the earliest in New Brunswick was in 1919 at St. Stephen where the Girl Guides gathered around a tree at the local hospital to sing carols. There must have been a local source of power, as the first

There is no question as to when the Alexander Gray family erected this tree, as the date is clearly displayed in the branches: 1921.

major supplier of electric power in the area was the Musquash Dam, built in 1921–22. Three years later, the Saint John High School Choir gathered around a brightly lit tree in uptown King's Square on Christmas Eve 1925. The newly formed Power Commission of the City of Saint John, which drew its power from the Musquash Dam, provided the lights. This same firm provided the first uptown decorative overhead Christmas lighting in 1951. These were intended to decorate the uptown for the visit of Princess Elizabeth and Prince Philip (then known as the Duke of Edinburgh) in early November of that year, but the merchants convinced city council to leave them up for the Yuletide season. In the following years, some of the merchants, especially on the so-called "Quality Block" on Germain Street, added to the original display, and it eventually spread throughout the city.

Just after the beginning of the twentieth century, the growth in those adding a tree to their Christmas decorating led to the establishment of the Christmas tree industry. According to a 1998 newsletter published by *The Tree House* of Fredericton and an article in the January 1973 issue of *Atlantic Advocate*, the first shipment of Christmas trees from New Brunswick to the Boston-area market occurred in 1905. Moe Cohan was the shipper, and he chose to send five railcars of balsam fir for sale in the US. *The Tree House* report noted, "Unfortunately, by the time they arrived in Boston, they were so tarnished with ashes and soot from the steam locomotive that they weren't very pretty."

Another early exporter was known as "The Christmas Tree Man," that being George L. LeBar, a Pennsylvania man cutting trees in King's County, New Brunswick. In 1948, he was described in the *King's County Record* as having been in the business for fifty-one years, starting in his home state in 1898, and beginning in 1908 to export trees from Hampton, New Brunswick. By 1919, the report continued, he was sending 265 railcars over the Canadian–US border. Many others got into the business as it became more and more popular to have a Christmas tree in the home. Today, the province has 350 growers, and about a half million trees are cut annually, with 85 percent of them going to the US market. Combined with some 4.5 million fir wreaths and grave blankets, New Brunswick has become the largest exporter of greenery in Canada.

The history of tree production in Nova Scotia, by contrast, dates back to 1914 or 1915, when The Bridgewater Bulletin in Lunenburg County noted on November 15, "A large number of Christmas trees are being stacked near the

The Chesley and Pidgeon family tree in their Douglas Avenue parlour in 1903.

railway station to be shipped to Boston." Contradicting this report is a Department of Natural Resources document that stated it was Arthur Manuel of Chester Station who made the first shipment in 1922 or 1923. Another report by R. R. Murray in 1948 fixed the date as 1932.

By 1957, a peak year for exports, Nova Scotia was exporting 3.8 million trees to the United States, Mexico, the Caribbean, South America, and even as far off as Japan. Lunenburg, Nova Scotia, calls itself the "Balsam Fir Christmas Tree Capital of the World," and nearly half of Nova Scotia's total Christmas tree production comes from this one county. Despite the introduction of artificial trees, the industry remains an important source of revenue for the province and in recent years, 1.3 million trees, valued at $35 million, have been cut and shipped annually.

One of the more bizarre stories connected with the shipments of trees occurred in early December 1931, when police somehow became suspicious of a truck travelling with what seemed to be a load of Christmas trees. They pulled the driver over, and under the trees they discovered twenty-two five-gallon kegs of rum destined for a bootlegger in the Halifax area.

The Forest, Fish and Wildlife Division of the Prince Edward Island provincial government says the province has a vibrant Christmas-tree industry, and enjoys a solid reputation for its fresh balsam wreaths, which are produced by some of its fourteen Christmas tree farmers. The Island operations are not export-orientated, but more focused on U-pick and local retail sales.

Newfoundland does not currently export any trees or wreaths, though twenty years ago they had some success with off-island sales. Today, there are half a dozen growers active in the province, which provide about 20 percent of homes with trees. Another 20 percent are imported from Nova Scotia. The local growers focus, like Prince Edward Island, on U-pick and local sales. Government incentives to encourage tree growing have been in place for decades, but have had limited success; it is still a time-honoured tradition in the province to go out and cut a wild tree on Crown land.

⤘⟨⟨⟨⟨⟩⟩⤙

Accounts of gathering around decorated trees in the first two decades of the twentieth century do not differ significantly from the last decades of the nineteenth century. It is in the twenties that the next major tree-related events occur, that being the erection of public trees in city squares and the gathering of the community to sing carols around these lit trees.

The first Atlantic Canadian city to offer this activity was Saint John, when singers gathered around a tree lit by the Power Commission on December 24, 1925, in the city centre, King's Square. The following year, Saint John High School alumni spearheaded the project, which was based on the idea of a carol sing around a community tree that began in Pasadena, California, in 1909, and had spread to Madison Square Park in New York by 1913. By 1924, public tree lightings became popular seasonal events in most major American cities.

Moncton followed Saint John's lead two years later, when the YMCA Men's Club sponsored a community tree lighting on December 22, 1927, at the corner of Main and Archibald Streets. The city's mayor, B. A. Taylor, threw a switch, and the *Moncton Times* reported, "A gasp of admiration came from the large crowd." The organizers had arranged for the words of familiar carols like "Hark, the Herald Angels Sing" and "O Come, All ye Faithful" to be flashed on a screen, and the local Salvation Army band accompanied the singers.

The first record of a community tree in Fredericton seems to be in 1935 when the YMCA erected a "brilliantly lighted tree," and arranged for several city choirs to lead carol singing under the direction of Professor W. F. Harrison. The *Gleaner*'s report of the event noted, "In spite of the near near-zero weather last night, a goodly number of citizens turned out and took part in the carol singing on the grounds of the Canadian Legion." The next year, in 1936, the *Gleaner* covered the event under the title "The Community Tree." The location changed to the "Provincial Normal School," and in addition to caroling led by Robert C. Bayley, Santa Claus was present and distributed "1,000 bags of mixed candy," which the report noted took from 7 to 8 P.M.

These community tree lightings happened in the heart of the depression years, but not in all communities, as some decided not to erect trees or hold public ceremonies due to the tight economic times. One of these was Woodstock, New Brunswick, whose town council in 1936 decided against erecting a community tree, even after having done so for several years. The citizens of the southern area of the town known as Wellington ward took the matter into their own hands and erected a tree at the foot of Universal Hill. A written account, which the *Daily Gleaner* received from a Woodstock writer, noted how effective the placement was, saying, "with the bright-colored lights illuminating Upper Main Street Hill, and the gaily lighted Christmas tree across the bridge, Woodstock has taken on a remarkable Christmas spirit outlook."

In Nova Scotia, there is a report of a community tree in Halifax in 1925, when it was noted in the *Saint John Globe* that in Halifax, "Christmas was celebrated this year in a greater measure than for some years past." It went on to note, "Thousands of dollars, publicly raised, were spent in bringing Christmas cheer to the unfortunates, and a huge community tree was set up in the Grand Parade and brightly illuminated. Christmas Eve, hundreds of the city's poor gathered about the tree and there was something for everybody. A regimental band played Christmas carols and choirs from the leading city churches sang the carols." In addition, the report noted: "There was a Christmas tree for horses set up in the old City Market Square, where the viands most appealing to the equine palate were scattered in abundance for every dobbin that chanced to approach the square." Certainly this would have been one of the more unusual trees set up publicly in the four provinces.

The next year, 1926, along the coast outside of Halifax, there was a "brilliantly lighted community tree" in front of the town hall in Liverpool, under the auspices of the Red Cross. Under the leadership of Reverend R. J. Porter, and accompanied by a number of town's choirs, carols were sung, concluding with "God Save the King."

The Irving community tree at the old burial ground in Saint John, New Brunswick, in the 1980s.

The idea of the community tree is still a popular part of seasonal celebrations across Atlantic Canada. One of the most spectacular in recent memory was the sixty-five-foot tree erected by the Irving Group of Companies in the Old Burial Ground in Saint John during the Bicentennial celebrations of the 1980s. As was the case in the earlier community tree events, choirs were invited to sing, not just for one night but through most of December. They would have had little trouble seeing the words to their carols, for the tree normally had over 7,500 lights. Unfortunately, the huge tree was the victim of windstorms on a couple of occasions, and as a consequence, a much shorter tree is now placed in the park-like city centre setting.

Saint John's most spectacular tree these days is not a tree at all, but strings of lights that give it the look of a tree at night. It is placed on Long Wharf each year, and one bulb is lit for every two-dollar donation received by the CBC, the sponsor, for the local food bank. While thousands are seasonally stirred by its brilliance, no one sings around its base, nor does Santa visit, due to its gated location on the harbourfront.

On Nova Scotia's South Shore there is another tree that is not really a tree, but is certainly a sight to behold: the Municipality of Barrington's Lobster Pot Tree. It stands on the waterfront of Cape Sable Island and consists of somewhere around two hundred recycled lobster pots stacked in a circle and rising up to a pinnacle, so it represents the shape of the traditional Christmas tree. More than one hundred of the pots are memorials to deceased fishermen of the area, while others represent boats currently out on the water. A huge star is placed at the very top of the traps, which are "decorated" with brightly painted lobster buoys and strings of lights. The display is deeply appreciated by members of the community, and even those who live far off now contribute to this effort by placing memorial buoys or traps.

There is no doubt that the best-known tree from eastern Canada is the Boston Christmas Tree, which was first sent in 1917, immediately after the Halifax Explosion, and then revived in 1971 and sent annually since then. The tree is a gift from the people of Nova Scotia to the people of Boston as a tribute for the aid received from the city following the Halifax explosion on December 6, 1917. This tragic event killed 2,000 people and injured 9,000, and destroyed two-thirds of downtown Halifax. The lighting ceremony on the Boston Common in 2017 received national coverage in the US and beyond, as it marked the disaster's one-hundredth anniversary. While the intent of the annual gift is ostensibly a tribute, the resulting publicity certainly helps Nova Scotia's annual sale of Christmas trees.

Prince Edward Island and Newfoundland and Labrador both have winter light shows that attract thousands of visitors during the dark days of late fall. In Charlottetown, three long-standing occasions have been melded into one busy weekend on the last Saturday in November: the Victorian Christmas Market, the Christmas Parade, the city's official

Tree Lighting ceremony. Discover Charlottetown, the weekend's organizers, felt that this joint approach would improve visitor numbers.

In St. John's, there are two principal places to enjoy the winter lights. Both are spectacular, but in different ways. At Bowring Park, the lights are set out around the Duck Pond; on being turned on, there are lots of choral groups to entertain and plenty of hot chocolate to be sipped. In town, there are sixty thousand lights on and around the Confederation Building. Both are lit by the first Saturday of December, and both shows continue until little Christmas on January sixth.

Not all tree stories are happy, however. In the early days of indoor trees, people adorned them with lit candles clipped onto the branches. Even though they were only lit for short periods of time and there were buckets of water or sand nearby in case of fire, accidents still happened. One such incident—of many which could be recounted—was reported in the *Saint John Standard* of January 2, 1914, under the headline "Candles on Xmas Tree Start Fire." It went on to report that a "serious blaze threatened Thomas Nixon's home last evening," and that Mr. Nixon was "severely burned on his face and hands." Through a call box system, the fire department was alerted promptly, and upon arrival "quickly subdued" the fire, and "the offending tree was thrown out on the street."

Though the first electric tree lights appeared in New York in 1882, they did not appear in homes in the Atlantic area for some years following. There is one anomaly, however, as Saint John resident Theophilus Cushing introduced electric tree lights in 1902, after having seen what were known as "fairy lights" on a trip to England. The Cushing lights were so popular that Theophilus's son, Travis Cushing, recalled in an interview some years ago, "Every Sunday school in the city would request them for their tree when they had closing parties."

During the Great Depression, New Brunswick children discovered that if they attached letters begging for food or gifts to the trees being shipped to American markets, someone might, in the spirit of the season, respond. It worked well for years and years. It is believed the practice originated in Quebec, but that is only supposition. When exactly the first letter was sent is also subject to debate, but it was almost certainly a depression practice, as evidenced by a story in the Fredericton *Gleaner* of December 26, 1934. It tells of a ten-year-old Northumberland County girl, Marie Ross Bolston, who attached a note to a tree, saying, "We are so poor we never have Santa come to see us, I am ten years old." The note was noticed by a clerk in a store in Richmond, Virginia, and with twenty others, put together a "box crammed with Christmas toys," and sent them off to Canada.

Some of those who wrote letters had their proverbial fifteen minutes of fame as a result. This was the case with Villa Matchett of Chatham, New Brunswick. Her 1947 letter ended up in Natchez, Mississippi, where the local paper published it. The Associated Press carried it on their wire service resulting in gifts and money being sent to her from all over the United States. When Radio Station CHSJ in Saint John learned of her good fortune, they arranged to fly her to the city, where *Telegraph Journal* reporter Ian Sclanders interviewed her about her experience. The publicity resulted in many more New Brunswick children sending off begging letters.

William Duthie of Miramichi, New Brunswick, pointed out that at least one marriage resulted from letters attached to trees. In a letter to this writer on December 14, 2011, he wrote: "I saw in the *Times & Transcript* you wanted to know about Xmas tree notes years ago. About 1948, a lad asked me to put a note in a bale of trees. I did. In January he told me he got a letter from a man in New York. His mother answered it and they were writing, and he came here to see them the next summer and kept coming back and they [the man and the mother] married and about a year after he and his two sisters moved to New York." In a subsequent interview, he gave the names of the individuals, but they did not want them published. Contact was made with family members still on the Miramichi to confirm his story, which they did, though they too requested no names be used.

Tree letters continued into the 1960s, when a rather embarrassing incident happened. Acting on a letter requesting help, a shipment of candy, fruit, and clothing arrived in Brantville, New Brunswick, from a US Air Force Base in Tampa, Florida. The shipment was left on the steps of the Tracadie Regional High School for distribution to area residents. Before local officials could pick it up, it was stolen. Upon hearing of the theft, the American airmen quickly rounded up more goodies and sent a second shipment. The incident received plenty of press, a lot of it negative. An editorial in the *Moncton Times*, for example, said "The Yuletide note appeals," is a "practice to be deplored," and "created a dark reflection on the province as a whole." It was the opinion of the editors that many who made appeals "greatly exaggerated their circumstances," and that steps should be taken so that the practice should "come to be pretty well abandoned

An engraved image of a typical tabletop Christmas tree, circa 1880s.

in the course of not too distant a time." Ministers, priests, and government officials came out against the idea, too, and so, as far as is known, it has come to be a thing of the past (or is done in complete secrecy).

Riverview resident Geralda Gallant was one of New Brunswick's children who benefited from placing a letter in a tree when she lived in Acadieville in the early 1950s. She received a doll for herself and her younger sister from a family in New Jersey. In addition, they stayed in touch by letter for years, right up to her graduation. "I think it was a good experience. The family in New Jersey felt good doing this, and we were so grateful, as we didn't have much at the time," she said. "I think the whole thing was ruined because people got too greedy."

This final paragraph will show the extent to which our ancestors went in greening their homes at Christmas. This woman's effort to decorate for the Christmas season seems more in tune with spring than winter, and it for sure was a bit over the top, even by Victorian standards. It was found in a scrapbook #C-27 on page 189 in the Saint John Regional Library. It was dated December 25, 1883:

> *A very unique decoration is that prepared by a lady who resides on Orange Street. While outside the walls of her residence, winter rules with his cold and icy hand, inside, everything betokens the existence of summer. The floors are covered with a rich green verdure, nature's own production. Trees and flowers*

appear in their summer hues, filling the room with their balmy odors; the birds sing merrily along the branches, apparently unaware of the deception that is being practiced upon them; a miniature lake teams with finny specimens, and even flies buzz as naturally as if summer were really here. The pleasant illusion has been the result of weeks of patient toil. The sods were lifted during the summer and nurtured with tender care until now. And so with the trees and plants. Those who have seen the decorations describe them as being both lovely and natural.

HOW SANTA CAME to ATLANTIC CANADA

⟿⟨ʘʘʘʘʘ⟩⟾

Few of those reading this book could imagine Christmas without Santa Claus, but his introduction to the Americas is actually just over two hundred years old. The European figure St. Nicholas, as he was known originally, is first mentioned in the New World in Washington Irving's *Knickerbocker's History of New York*, published in 1809. Irving noted New York citizens were not keen on the celebration of Christmas and his hope was to have the residents lighten up and enjoy a more festive and secular celebration. He had St. Nicholas flying over New York, seated in a horse-drawn wagon, and dropping presents to the city's children.

In 1821, likely based on Irving's ideas, a New York Presbyterian minister named Arthur J. Stansbury wrote a book titled *The Children's Friend*. It was fully illustrated and, unusual for the era, published in full colour. The pictures showed St. Nicholas with a single reindeer pulling his sleigh full of rewards to be dropped into stockings for good boys and girls (and switches for the stockings of those who had misbehaved). It is unlikely

Evening Telegram

St. John's, December 24, 1896.

"A MERRY CHRISTMAS!"

The December 24, 1896, issue of St. John's Evening Telegram.

children in Atlantic Canada saw this book, as only two are known to exist, so it's unlikely it was widely distributed.

However, the next year, Clement Clarke Moore's "A Visit from St. Nicholas" was written, even though it was meant to be read strictly for his family at their Chelsea Mansion in what is now central New York City. The following year, one of Moore's relatives sent it to the *Troy Sentinel*, and it got printed for all subscribers to enjoy. Thereafter, it spread rapidly across America and into Canada (it was first published in the *New Brunswick Courier* on December 25, 1830.) It is in this twenty-eight verse poem that the single reindeer of Stansbury's 1821 book became eight, and received names. St. Nicholas takes on a more jocund appearance as well, but still looks very saintly; though he has a long way to go before his image matches the "jolly old elf" we consider Santa today.

It was 1848 before this poem appeared in book form with illustrations so until then, children reading the piece had formed their own impression of the saint's appearance. Though there were Canadian publications—for instance: *Juvenile Magazine* (1847–1851) out of Montreal—circulating in the Atlantic region, no images of the old gent appeared until the 1880s.

At this time, many merchants would advertise as if Santa himself were present in their establishment. Slogans like: "Santa Claus headquarters," "Hard to beat old reliable Santa Claus," or "Come and see Father Christmas," appeared in bold type in shop windows, and were followed by a list of the various goods the merchant had supposedly gotten from Santa himself.

Postcard showing how Santa kept up to date by using automobiles in the second decade of the twentieth century.

With the exception of Manchester Robertson Allison's department store, there is nothing to indicate a live costumed Santa was present in stores in Atlantic Canada in the 1880s. Occasionally, the editorial copy that newspapers of the era provided for their advertisers would indicate that the store window had a display that featured an *image* of Santa. This was the case in Halifax's People's Store in 1882, when it was reported "a life-like figure of the venerable dispenser of Christmas toys and candies" could be seen at the Gottingen Street store. Gradually through the 1880s, advertisers added an image of Santa to their promotions, with the earliest seeming to have been in the *Fredericton Capital* in 1882. It featured an engraving taken from the first edition of Clement Moore's poem "A Visit from St. Nicholas," and showed Santa on a rooftop carrying a sack of parcels, about to venture down a chimney.

By 1890, there were so many versions of Santa in newspaper illustrations that it must have been confusing for children to get a grip on just what the benevolent chap looked like. Some were copies of the one image that is considered to have established once and for all just what Santa

Santa descends into a Fredericton chimney in this sketch, seemingly copied from the 1848 illustrated edition of A Visit From St. Nicholas. *It is the first image of Santa to appear in an Atlantic Canadian newspaper, and was in the* Fredericton Capital *of December 23, 1882.*

looked like. That was Thomas Nast's depiction, which appeared on *Harper's Illustrated Weekly* covers every December from 1862 to 1886.

While Nast may have standardized the pictorial image, judging by the few photos of live Santas from the mid-1880s, most children would not be anxious to crawl up on his knee and share their hopes for Christmas gifts. It would seem that whatever could be secured would do as a costume. Usually, his face was covered with a mask; sometimes there was a beard, and other times no facial hair at all. Newspaper reports of Santa's visits note they were mostly at Sunday school gatherings after December 25. Normally, the person playing the role of Santa was identified, though the children may not have been aware of this when they met Santa in person.

The answer to the question of when Santa impersonators first showed up in each of the provinces is open to speculation (except for the story of confectioner Charles A. Sampson from New Brunswick). A careful reading of area newspapers, however, yields what appears to be the first in the three other Atlantic provinces. The earliest was on Prince Edward Island, where a January 1, 1885, report in the *Summerside Journal* noted: "There were three hundred children entertained at dinner at Ludlow Hall on Friday last (December 26) by some of the good people of the town. After ample justice had been done to the repast, Santa Claus made his appearance and distributed several hundred prizes among the children from two heavily laden Christmas trees."

Newfoundland appears to have been next: on December 12, 1888, a live Santa, his wife at his side, appeared at a festival at the George Street United Church in St. John's. The couple followed up the next week with appearances on Wednesday and Thursday at a bazaar at St. Thomas's Schoolroom. Five years pass before another live Santa is reported by the December 23, 1893, issue of the *Evening Telegram*, which reported, "Old Mr. Claus came out and presented the little ones with their presents off the tree," at the Congregational Band of Hope gathering at the Monkstown Training School.

Nova Scotia seems to have been the last of the provinces to have a visit from a live Santa. It finally occurred at the Dumb and Deaf Institution in Halifax on December 28, 1891. As the *Morning Herald* reported it, the children of the school were "keeping a sharp lookout" for the old gent, and were "thrown into a state of excitement by the sudden and unceremonious arrival of Father Christmas puffing and blowing under the weight of a sack of well filled stockings." His arrival, the report noted, "had created a certain amount of apprehension on the faces of the little ones," but when Santa flashed a kindly smile and began to "sign and spell fluently" for the children, he became a welcome figure at the party.

These days, Santa visits communities much earlier in December and appears in many more public places and events than was the case in the Victorian era.

At MRA's when Santa began his appearances is 1887, the fact that children took advantage of the opportunity to visit Santa is clear from a December 24 snippet in the *Daily Telegraph*, which read: "A five-year-old pride of the family has visited MRA's store and she came home with her eyes bright and her cheeks rosy with delight. 'I saw Santa Claus,' she announced, 'and it was the real live Santa Claus too! He crossed his legs and sat on the chimney and frew a kiss at me and I frew a kiss at him.'"

When department-store Santas became the norm is not clear from reading old papers, as Santa's visit is often included as part of their promotions, but there is scant evidence of when and where he actually appeared. What is clear, though, is that by the late 1920s it was a fixture of toy lands in larger stores.

⋘⟨ᴏᴏᴏᴏ⟩⋙

The first Santa Claus Parade in eastern Canada was in Saint John, New Brunswick, in November 1951, when Manchester Robertson Allison's department store and the Jaycees sponsored the event on the third Saturday of the month. The tradition has continued to this day, though MRA's ceased to operate (and thus, sponsor) in 1973. The 2018 parade will be number sixty-eight.

Halifax had its first holiday parade in 1995, though there were earlier "Santa parades" as is obvious from an article in the Halifax *Chronicle Herald* of December 7, 1995, which stated: "This is the first time in approximately 30 years that there has been a parade in the downtown area." One of the unique facets of the parade was a float where all the Santas who had participated in the earlier Santa look-alike contest rode together on a flatbed. This might have been confusing to the children, except it was pointed out that "the real Santa, accompanied by Miss Canadian International, Jody Cook, would bring up the rear in a horse-drawn carriage."

In Charlottetown, the parade is stated to be twentieth and in St. John's it will be the sixty-fifth. In both provinces there have been earlier parades that the older residents recall, but there is, for various reasons, no official record that can be consulted to give an accurate indication of just what transpired prior to the current count.

According to an article in the St. John's *Evening Telegram* of November 19, 1979, the Junior Chamber of Commerce and the Avalon Mall were the original joint sponsors of the holiday parade. One of the unique facets of this parade was that one hundred clowns collected children's letters to Santa Claus and deposited them into waiting Canada Post trucks, which were also part of the parade. The week after the parade in 1979, a competing mall arranged for Santa to be present on train trips, causing a brief revival of the Terra Transport service that linked St. John's with Kilbride Crossing. The event, which accommodated 120 children, was dubbed the "Santa Express."

In all of these instances, there seems to have been earlier public Santa events—some in connection with malls, others with service clubs—in which he arrived in some sort of parade or community event. These were not consistent, though numerous people interviewed recalled them happening in their youth. Thus, parades and public Santa appearances go back some years before website records would indicate.

CHURCH ACTIVITY REMAINS TRUE to OLD-TIME CHRISTMAS

‑ᴏᴏᴏᴏᴏ‑

If someone from the late nineteenth century could come for a visit today, he or she would likely find the modern church's way of marking the season similar in many ways to his or her own experience, but would also find plenty of stark differences. Perhaps this individual would agree with the sentiment "Christmas has become too commercial," and would align themselves with the Church's idea that "Christ" should be put back into "Christmas."

Even though we are certainly living in a more secular era, churches still fill up for Christmas services and events. Bazaars, teas, craft sales, and special musical presentations are still offered by many churches over the holidays, and are still well supported. It's hard to say just what draws people to Christmas Eve and Christmas Day masses and services, but possibly

This is the earliest depiction of the birth of Christ in Atlantic papers, and is from the Fredericton Capital *of December 1884.*

it is nostalgia; remembering a time when life seemed more controlled than it does at present.

Certainly the age-old services, children's pageants, choral presentations, and sacred surroundings provide a moving and deeply spiritual window to the past. This visitor from the 1880s would, however, note some differences in addition to the many similarities in the modern Christmas church experience.

The scripture readings, for example, are exactly as they were; there is no need to change the timeless story of Jesus's birth in Bethlehem, with the visit of the angels, shepherds, and wise men, and King Herod's evil plot to kill the newborn Son of God.

The music, which often tells the same story in another way, has not changed to any degree either. Snippets of music from Handel's *Messiah*, Bach's "Oratorio," and a half-dozen other classical composers that were popular in the Victorian era, remain popular to this day, despite the evolution of musical tastes.

The hymns sung at modern Christmas services were largely composed in the 1800s, or earlier. Though there is lots of new sacred Christmas music composed for and performed by choral groups, nothing has come along to replace time-honoured classics. There is the over three-hundred-year-old "While Shepherds Watched Their Flocks by Night," or the equally old "O Come, All ye Faithful"; James Montgomery's "Angels from the Realms of

Angel chorus from McGee's, 1878.

Glory" is also hundreds of years old, and the ever-popular "Silent Night" was written almost two hundred years ago, to name just a few.

One detail that might surprise a yesteryear visitor would be the surplices worn by robed choirs, especially in Anglican churches. Considered popish by Protestants, the white robes did not become popular in non-Roman Catholic churches until the turn of the twentieth century. However, in many churches today, praise bands provide the music for services and do not don surplices.

Another surprise would be the decorations. In the Victorian era, only Anglicans decorated with greenery extensively. Most other Protestants did not even hold services unless Christmas Day happened to fall on a Sunday. Poinsettias would also seem strange to a visitor from the nineteenth century. Though Victorians knew the plants since Joel Poinsett introduced them as a Christmas decoration in 1829, they were not widely used in church decorations until the 1950s.

Since seemingly little has changed over the decades, it is understandable that modern church celebrations might be overlooked by many. This is evidenced by the press coverage, which is practically nil now compared to what appeared in the papers decades ago. So let's compare some of the aspects of Atlantic Canadian celebrations of yesteryear with current ones.

Prior to the twentieth century, it was the Anglicans who decorated most lavishly, using native greens. In 1888, accounts in the *Saint John Globe* for example, describe St. John's (Stone) Church in Saint John, New Brunswick, to have been decorated with so much spruce that the gallery was almost hidden. St. James Anglican Church across town on Broad Street was described as having a triple arch of spruce in the nave. Trinity Anglican Church had "green-entwined pillars and great wreaths of spruce," and it was noted that the church was long considered the "best decorated in the city."

At Saint John's Cathedral of the Immaculate Conception—then as now on Waterloo Street—there was much less decorative material used, as staunch Catholics believed the greenery took away from the "solemn appearance" of the cathedral. The church was not totally bare of decoration, however, as there was some pine arranged around various statues, and the altar was garnished with spruce. Among the greenery, tiny flickering candles made the scene "quietly attractive" according to a *Saint John Globe* newspaper report of the era. At St. Peter's Catholic Church in the city's north end, a crèche, or nativity scene, was on display, considered to be "representative of the stable at Bethlehem...showing the God child in the manger." It was described as a "very tasteful piece of work." At that time, only Roman Catholic churches had such depictions of the Christmas story, though now it has become a part of the Christmas decorative effort of almost every denomination.

In PEI, the December 31, 1885, issue of the *Summerside Journal* reported: "The new Episcopal church at Port Hill was elaborately decorated for Christmas Day. There was a good attendance considering the bad state of the roads. A collection was taken up, the proceeds of which amounted to $20.00. The choir rendered some nice music." Unfortunately, just what was sung is not mentioned in this report, or in many others in Prince Edward Island papers.

Around this time, advertisements for church craft and bake sales started boasting of their "Xmas Trees," because trees were still such rarities

"Glory to God in the Highest. On Earth, Peace; Goodwill to Men" from the Halifax Herald *of December 24, 1898.*

in homes. The *Charlottetown Examiner* of December 18, 1888, carried an advertisement for the Ladies of St. Joseph's Convent, who were holding a sale on "Tuesday, 18th inst." The advertisement stated: "Besides the 'XMAS TREE' and 'FANCY WORK TABLE,' there will also be 'REFRESHMENTS' and well supplied 'TEA TABLES.'" Said refreshments included oysters and ice cream, which could be enjoyed while listening to St. Dunstan's College Band. Admission was ten cents.

Newfoundland's *Carbonear Herald* of December 25, 1879, recorded a most unusual event for the era, it being the first community noted to have a Christmas service broadcast by telephone. It went from the Dominion

Methodist Church to the residence of the manager of the Dominion Telegraph Company who handled the broadcast, making it available to an invalid citizen, so he, while reclining on a couch, with others gathered in his home, could hear clearly the entire service, including the sermon and the choral singing.

Although greenery was not explicitly described in Newfoundland papers, the music was—and there was a decidedly high level of music at St. John's churches in the 1880s. An advertisement in the December 24, 1888, issue of the *Evening Telegram* stated that on Christmas Day, "A-MUSICAL-TREAT" would be sung and would include selections from Mendelssohn, Handel, and Gounod. The program was to be held at 4:30 P.M. at St. Andrew's Presbyterian Church—colloquially known as The Kirk—with singers of St. Andrew's supported by five members of the St, Andrews Church Musical Association as soloists. This "musical treat" was performed four years after Handel's *Messiah* was sung in Newfoundland for what appears to have been the first time at the Athenaeum—a combination library, auditorium, and museum. (Although not a religious event, it's likely members of various church choirs made up the St. John's Choral Society, who performed at the Athenaeum under the direction of E. Handcock in 1884.)

Despite the promise of good music, it was Santa Claus and his wife who were the novel attraction at the Festival at George Street Church in 1888. According to the report in the St. John's *Evening Times* of December 13, there was a poor turnout despite the rare opportunity to see the old gent and his wife.

In Nova Scotia, decorating churches was well established by the late 1860s. A report in the *Evening Reporter* of December 26, 1874, read: "The different Episcopalian churches in this city [Halifax] were decorated yesterday with evergreens, mottos, etc." (In that era, it was not permissible to decorate until after the fourth Sunday of Advent, which in 1874 fell just one day before Christmas.) The report continued: "The Round Church [St. George's] displayed remarkably good taste. Indeed this church has been for years noted for this fact. Of course, to the ladies belongs the principal portion of the credit for this, and it is therefore cheerfully accorded them."

In addition to insight about the greenery and decorations, the *Dartmouth Patriot* of December 28, 1901, allows a look into the church music of the day. It noted that "carols will be sung at the conclusion of the regular

Pennfield Christmas party, 1960.

service" at the Christ Church on Dundas Street in Dartmouth the following Sunday night. The choir would render special numbers, including: "All This Night," "Once in Bethlehem," and "Angels from the Realms" by Maunder; "Sleep, Holy Babe" by Dykes; "Like Silver Lamps" by Stadgal; "Ring out the Bells" by Hodges; "When Christ was Born" by Brown; "O Little Town of Bethlehem" by Nevin, and "O, Holy Night" by Adam. The latter is still among the most popular carols on many Christmas programs to this day.

Christmas bazaars were held in Halifax from the early 1870s onwards, and were successful enough that various churches could place newspaper

A typical church pageant with costumed characters telling the Christmas story, possibly at Waterloo Street Baptist Church in Saint John, New Brunswick.

advertisements the same size as the leading merchants of the city. (These were still small by today's standards, however: about one column wide by two or three inches high.) One such ad in the *Daily Reporter* ran for the Brunswick Street Tabernacle on December 16, 1878, and in bold type told of their "BAZAAR and CHRISTMAS TREES!" In tiny eye-straining type, it noted it had trees "already trimmed and ready for sale from .50 cents to $5.00." Tea was available for ".30 cents, and oysters for .25 cents." As added attractions there were: "Pharaoh's Serpents, White Mice, fish the pastor caught and stuffed in England, a Model Steam Engine and Boiler (thought to be the smallest in Halifax), working with a full pressure of steam." The church was creative in its efforts, as it had to be, for the papers were full of such promotions in every town and city of the Atlantic area.

Churches to this day make a concerted effort to bring the message of Christmas to those who visit by decorating, with musical events, through pageants, with teas and food-related events, with outreach programs for the less fortunate. They may differ in how they are structured, but our visitor from the past, who opened this look at the festive season in the church, would likely fit in quite readily, and adapt quite quickly to the church's efforts of the current times.

CHRISTMAS GAMES of YESTERYEAR, ATLANTIC STYLE

~~~~~

Games at Christmas in the late 1800s were not at all like the games children play on their electronic devices today. For the most part, they were interactive, very physical, and involved a mix of ages, which fit the times perfectly. Most families in this period were quite large, and had several generations living under the same roof. This was also a period when visiting to see what was under the tree from Santa was the norm.

What didn't differ from each other were the games played all across North America at Christmas and New Year. Many of the games were very old, and originated in the English celebration of the season. From the early 1880s, the widely circulated American magazine *St. Nicholas* was found in many households with children, as it was considered the very best Christmas reading for young minds. Bookstores also carried many periodicals from Britain like *Godey's Lady Book and Magazine*, the *Strand*, and *Holly Leaves*, to name just three, which all published Christmas articles that featured games, crafts, and stories by top writers of the day. As copyright laws were not rigidly enforced, most daily newspapers simply copied out what they thought would be of interest to the local readers, sometimes changing the copy to reflect local conditions.

Under the headline "Amusements for Christmas Night," the widely circulated *Family Herald* gave the following advice as a way to open a night of game playing: "On the arrival of guests, they will each be presented with a colored favour. On entering the dining room, an enormous bran pie will be discovered in the middle of the table from which colored ribbons descend. Each guest chooses the ribbon that matches his favour, and draws out a Christmas gift."

The article then went on to suggest two games, "The Battle of the Roses" and "Christmas Bells," both of which required some preparation on the part of the host. The "Battle of the Roses" was basically a competition between two teams, one with cutouts of red roses, the other cutouts of white roses, which they pelted at one another as they ran about the room trying to reach a safe zone without being hit by a rose. "Christmas Bells" required a piano, and a piano player, and most homes had both in the Victorian era. The children were outfitted with bells, all of a distinctive note. The children were seated on chairs or couches around the living room and when the piano sounded the note that matched their bell, they had to jump up and run around the couch and chairs and try to seat themselves before the pianist could tag them.

However, these were not the most popular games of the Christmas season. That title belonged to "Snapdragon." It seems a strange game today (and would certainly not be allowed to be played in any home) but appeared annually in newspapers of the era and frequently in magazines circulated throughout Atlantic Canada. One of these papers that carried "Snapdragon" instructions was the *Saint John Globe* of December 24, 1879. It began: "There are some games that seem to belong particularly to Christmas and foremost among these is the game of 'Snapdragon':

Here he comes with his flaming bowl
Don't he mean to take his toll?
Snip! Snap! Dragon!

Take care you don't take too much,
Be not greedy to your clutch,
Snip! Snap! Dragon!

With his blue and lapping tongue
Many of you will be stung,
Snip! Snap! Dragon!
For he snaps at all who comes
Snatching at his feast of plums,
Snip! Snap! Dragon!

But old-Christmas makes him come,
Though he looks so fee! fa! fum!
Snip! Snap! Dragon!
Don't fear him, but be bold,
Out he goes, his flames are cold,
Snip! Snap! Dragon!

To play "Snapdragon," a number of raisins are put in a large, broad, shallow bowl and a little brandy or other spirit is poured over the fruit and ignited. The lights in the room are then extinguished, and the players take turns plunging their hands through the flames, trying to grab the raisins. This, of course, was not easy; it required both nerve and agility and the unavailing attempts of the company caused a good deal of fun. Added to this, the burning spirit would give off a lurid glare, which lit up the eager faces of the players, giving them strange shadows and effects.

The article went on to explain that the game "has been played at Christmas from time immemorial," perhaps dating back to Hercules when he "had slain the flaming dragon of Hesperia," and then used apples grown in a nearby orchard for the fruit to be snapped out of the flaming bowl. The article added: "Some games, which are rather boisterous in their character are known to everyone and need no description. Among these are 'Blind Man's Buff,' 'Puss in the Corner,' 'Trencher,' 'Blind Postman,' 'Hunt the Slipper,' 'The Elements,' or 'Earth, Air, Fire and Water.'" Some of these are certainly readily identifiable and still played to this day, while others have faded into obscurity.

Snapdragon.

One in particular, "Blind Man's Buff," also appeared annually, was played with vigour in many a home, and would still be playable to this day. (Note the game mentioned here is variously spelled "Buff" or "Bluff.") Like "Snapdragon," it has been played since ancient times. There are many variations of the game, which began as an outdoor diversion said to have been modelled after a brave warrior who lost his sight during battle. The solider insisted on being led into the thick of the fighting and died flailing his sword at the enemy. This led to a military exercise where a blindfolded warrior, brandishing a blunt weapon, would try to fight all those who would challenge him. Soon the custom spread, and children, who then, as now, loved to imitate adult behaviour, cottoned on quickly. Thus a game developed where one lad would be blindfolded and armed, and the other boys would try to keep out of his way by hiding behind trees, rocks, buildings, or whatever might provide a suitable hiding spot.

When the game moved indoors is anybody's guess, but by Victorian times, it was indeed a popular parlour game, and especially popular as an after-supper diversion following Christmas dinner. By then a new element had been added: co-ed players. The occasions for a gentleman and lady to enjoy one another's company under the guise of play were few and far

"He could imitate Punch and Judy"

Punch and Judy shows were popular at-home entertainment.

between. It became the subject of much suspicion when a gentleman was always able to find the prettiest lady in the group despite being blind-folded, and often there were suggestions that hoods, and not blindfolds, should be used in the game, as was done in the beginning.

One of the many alternative versions of "Blind Man's Buff" that solved these perceived decency issues is the version children seem to enjoy most today. In this version, the blindfolded "buff" holds a short stick, while the others circulate the room, singing and dancing. Buff shouts "stop" and all players freeze. Buff then reaches out with the stick, touching someone, and that person must repeat "good morning" (or some such phrase) three times. Voice disguises are allowed, and if the buff can correctly identify the person, he is relieved of his blindfold, and that person takes his place; if not, he must continue his role.

Besides those games mentioned above, "Charades" and "Proverbs" were also popular parlour games at Christmastime. "Charades" is still a well-known game; Proverbs probably needs some description. To play, one person leaves the room while the rest choose a familiar proverb. The banished one returns and questions each person, who must answer the questions using one word from the proverb in a proper sequence. In a variation, the banished one returns to the room and shouts, "ready, aim, fire!" The others simultaneously shout the words of the proverb they had been assigned. The resulting sound is a confusing one the banished player must decipher and piece together to guess the proverb.

Most readers need not be told how to play "Simon Says" or "Musical Chairs" or "Twenty Questions," though many may not realize these too were popular parlour pastimes one hundred, and even two hundred, years ago. "Russian Scandal," on the other hand, needs to be explained. As it appeared in the *Globe*, it sounds like an interesting game to try. One player writes a short story on a slate, making it as full of incidents as he can. He then steps outside, calls one of his companions to join him, and reads him the story aloud once, very distinctly. The storyteller then walks away, taking the slate with him. The person to whom the story was read summons another of the party, and narrates the story to him as exactly as he can remember. The third person tells it to the fourth, the fourth to the fifth, and so on until each one playing has had the story narrated to him privately and solemnly outside the door. When all have heard it, the last one to go out comes back into the room and narrates the story to the whole company. The original is then read from the slate, and it is quite curious to notice how it has altered in the course of transmission. This, of course, is a longer version of the modern game "Telephone."

Games in which others were made the fool of were as popular in olden times as they are today. In "Brother, I'm Bobbed," for example, two people who were "in" on the stunt sit in two chairs at opposite ends of a line of three chairs. A sheet was thrown over their heads. A victim was brought in from outside and sat down in the middle chair, also covered with a sheet. The victim thought the three of them were to guess who was knocking them on the head and if he guessed correctly, he would be taken out from under the sheet. In reality, the two sitting on either side of him were doing the knocking, but they had to pretend they too were getting knocked, so the victim would guess from among the others in the room. The fun continued until the victim caught on.

In another tricky game, a victim was shown a candle placed plainly in view on a table. After being blindfolded and twisted around a few times, he was then challenged to find the candle and blow it out. That alone provided some great amusement, but if the blindfolded one proved astute, then the candle was removed altogether, and he or she could be seen puffing at the air for some considerable time before the hoax was exposed.

Of course, these are but a few of the games enjoyed in times past, but enough to give an idea of some family-room fun that would have been enjoyed by generations of children, and which should provide a way to link Christmas today with Christmas of long ago.

OUTDOOR ENJOYMENT at CHRISTMAS LONG AGO

࿊

The Christmas period could readily be called the *S* season when we consider the wide range of outdoor pursuits beginning with the letter *S*: on the positive side we have snowmen, sliding, snowshoeing, skiing, sledding, sleigh riding, snowshoeing, skating, and snowballing, and on the negative side slipping and shivering. Indeed, the pursuits themselves have not changed greatly over the decades, but participation at Christmastime certainly has. Though most could be even more enjoyable today (with improved equipment and warmer clothing), they just aren't as popular at Christmas as they once were; sleigh riding has all but disappeared.

Let's look back and see how and where these wintery pastimes were enjoyed in the olden days.

Christmas skating postcard.

♂Saint John, New Brunswick

In 1877, the year of the Great Fire of Saint John, there was a great interest in outdoor pursuits during the Christmas season. "Skating was indulged in by the lads in the King's Square, as well as upon many of the streets," was the *Daily Telegraph*'s comment on December 21, 1877. Those who could get to Lily Lake could enjoy the ice there, but they would have to share the surface with curlers (the bachelors always played the married men on Christmas afternoon). In the days immediately following Christmas, the ice-cutting operators would be busy pulling huge blocks of ice out for use the following summer. Snowshoeing in the wilds surrounding Lily Lake was similarly popular. Those who were able to hire sleighs for the day might go out to what was called "the Chalet" on the Kennebecasis River and enjoy skating over to Long Island. Other sleigh riders would choose to travel fourteen miles eastward and hold a supper and dance at Ben Lomond House or Johnstone's Hotel on the shores of Loch Lomond Lake. In town, sliding and skiing were enjoyed on a number of city hills, or even on designated steep city streets, which were closed to traffic so youngsters could enjoy zipping down them. The Keewaydin Snowshoe Club, which ran from Millidge Avenue over the Rockland Road Hill to the Paradise Row area, also owned a giant toboggan for public use. Certainly there was no lack of opportunity for outdoor adventures, though there was only a

Lights in uptown Saint John, circa 1970s.

fifty-fifty chance of a white Christmas in Saint John, and as reported in 1877: "The absence of snow made it [Christmas] in some respects very dull."

Fredericton, New Brunswick

The diary of Lady Jane Hunter—wife of Sir Martin Hunter, who was stationed in Fredericton with the British Militia in the first decade of the nineteenth century—provides the earliest record of outdoor leisure activities during winter. Lady Hunter wrote letters back to her native England, containing vivid descriptions of their home in New Brunswick, military life, and social activities. On November 1, 1804, she wrote: "Our gay season does not commence until after Christmas, when the river gets quite frozen over, and then everybody is flying about on sleighs." In another letter, she notes: "It is a very pleasant and most expeditious mode of travelling."

Lady Hunter does not mention curling, but it is known that this sport began on the same ice she enjoyed in 1854, as the founder of the game, John Neill, was honoured in 1883 when he was declared the oldest curler in the province. That year, he delivered a "model shot" to begin a day-long open-ice tournament on Christmas Day: married men versus bachelors. According to a report in the *Fredericton Capital* on January 3, 1884, the married men won the tournament that day, 66–47. Later in the evening, the public was invited to take to the ice and skate to the music of the Fredericton Brass Band; three hundred locals took advantage of the invitation.

Another invitation Frederictonians accepted was the challenge of swooshing down the 150-foot toboggan slide built on the green just opposite the legislative building in 1886 and opened on Christmas Day that year. "Away you go," was the headline of the Fredericton *Gleaner*. It noted that there was a "commodious waiting room," which was "reached by a broad flight of stairs," that led to the top of the slide, which had a slope ratio of one foot in three. "Gentleman could obtain season tickets, or just some for the afternoon for 50 cents," the report noted, which would "allow a gentleman to take with him as many lady companions as he chooses." D. J. Stockford was the man in charge, and he was quoted as having said he would do "all in his power to assist the parties on the slide in having a jolly time."

Moncton, New Brunswick

A December 24, 1877, comment in the *Daily Times* showed that the Hub City, which was then just a town, was not much different from other areas of the provinces in its outdoor pursuits. It began, "Christmas tomorrow promises to be a lively day in Moncton," and followed this with copy about the religiously disposed and the possibilities of church services, before adding, "others will seek innocent amusement in recreation and sleigh driving, skating etc." The piece concluded, "The owners of fast and slow teams will be rejoiced to observe that sleighing is likely to be very good, while those who find enjoyment on the skates will be glad to know that the rink is in excellent condition and will be open during the whole day. It is expected the rink will be attractive during Christmas and particularly during the evening." This was the Columbia Rink.

One of the most unusual Christmas season outings for Moncton children occurred on Boxing Day of 1904. At that time, it was not yet a holiday, and to entice crowds of shoppers to his post-Christmas sales, merchant L. Higgins, who ran a boot and shoe store, threw "$20.00 in coppers," from the second floor window of his establishment. There was a "large crowd,"

Band on sleigh in Chatham, New Brunswick (Provincial Archives of New Brunswick, PA P 18/34).

of small boys, and "girls also joined in the scramble." One lad who showed up with a barrel to catch the falling pennies was jostled away by other kids. Adults watched the event with "amusement" for the hour it took the children to round up all two thousand coins. It was "pretty cold work digging in the snow," one youth commented, but the writer of the piece concluded that "Mr. Higgins's name was on the lips of every youth present...and he made himself more popular than ever with the rising population."

Prince Edward Island

The *Summerside Journal* of January 1, 1880, reported that Christmas Day of 1879 the "weather was very fine, clear and frosty" and the "sleighing was excellent." There were those who participated in "snowshoeing and various other amusements," many apparently just walking about as "the sidewalks all day long [were] literally black with people." However, there was a negative side to the day, as the number of "drunks" was "larger than on former occasions," and "small boys were seen reclining about the streets and apparently trying to raise a row."

At Christmas in 1885, the *Summerside Journal* wished the Crystal Rink a successful season upon its opening, which, of course, depended on the cold weather setting in. The paper's column explained the rink was one of the "largest and best appointed in the provinces," and had a surface of 140 feet by 50 feet with excellent dressing rooms and a bandstand.

In Charlottetown, the *Patriot* noted the opening of the Hillsborough Rink just three days before Christmas in 1893, but regretted that though there was "splendid conditions and good music furnished by Galbraith's band," the attendance was "not up to the mark." The entry ended with speculation, noting, "This is to be wondered at, considering what a healthful pastime skating is." The paper, being full of merchant's inducements to shoppers, may have been the reason staring them right in the face.

In 1898, the same rink opened the day following Christmas, and advertised: "Parents can send their children to the rink this winter without any fear of the little ones being hurt as the manager (A. A. Bartlett) will make it his personal business to see that no rowdyism is allowed on the ice." Prices for membership were stated as "Gentleman $3.50; Ladies $2.50; and Children $1.50." Translated into 2018 dollars, this would be over $100.00 for the gentleman.

Halifax, Nova Scotia

Perhaps the most obvious place for outdoor winter enjoyment in Halifax was Citadel Hill, as it was, and is, impossible to visit or live in the city without being aware of this dominating downtown hill. The slope has always been popular with youngsters for sliding, and this was sometimes a problem police had to deal with. The coasters progressed at considerable speed onto city streets, which would frighten passing horses.

For the adults, the Citadel itself was a popular place for an outing between Christmas and New Year, as reported by the *Daily Reporter* of December 26, 1877. In that year, the 97th Regiment of British men had decorated the garrison, and the *Reporter* noted, "a prettier sight is rarely—indeed never—seen in Halifax. The band room looks like a fairy palace." The public was cautioned, however, that the display would only be open for visits until New Year's Day.

Christmas Eve of 1888 was a night of "balmy weather," and brought out the "maids, youth, and children" of the city to walk the downtown street in "perfectly clear weather with a myriad of stars brightly shining. The principal thoroughfares were densely thronged...there was lots of good cheer, everybody seemed good natured and jovial," the writer of the *Morning Chronicle* wrote in the December 25 edition. "All were intent, apparently on enjoying themselves or planning for others' enjoyment." The highlight of the evening was that the Chandler Electric Company had a display of incandescent lights in the window of their premises on Granville Street. There were different styles of globes and shades, with the most novel feature being a light in a large glass vessel that was filled with water. The piece concluded by saying when turning from the electric light, "the stores adjoining with gas presented a dingy appearance."

So entrenched was skating as a Christmas attraction that the *Halifax Herald* of December 26, 1899, headed up a column reviewing the previous day with the sensational "NO SKATING FOR CHRISTMAS." It went on to note, "Christmas was quietly celebrated in Halifax. Rain fell most inconveniently in the morning, but the sun came out at noon and made the afternoon much more attractive for the holiday. Skating was discounted by the weather. There has been no snow. Walking was not the best so it was a day for indoor observance." The Halifax Common was another popular outdoor skating location that would have been great for walking on that Christmas of 1899, but there would have been no skating.

Across the harbour in Dartmouth, the Snow-Shoe Club usually held its annual meeting at the Creighton home just around Christmas and would have been looking forward to tramps out to the lakes Dartmouth is famous for, but with no snow, this too would have been scrapped.

St. John's, Newfoundland

Unlike the sledding, skiing, snowshoeing, and skating of the other three Atlantic provinces around Christmastime, a most unusual outdoor event

Another of artist Edward J. Russell's sketches in the Daily Telegraph *in 1894, showing a typical seasonal sleighing outing.*

is reported in the St. John's *Evening Telegram* of 1890. On Boxing Day, a "FOOTBALL MATCH between the Star and St. Andrew's teams" on the St. Andrew's grounds ended in a draw, with each side having scored a goal. This same issue reported a more normal Christmas event: skating on the lower end of Quidi Vidi Lake, and indicated "quite a number of the boys indulged," even though it was declared that the "upper part of the lake, especially the middle, was not frozen solidly." Skaters were sometimes too anxious to get out on the ice, as can be seen in a report on December 26, 1890—in the *St. John's Daily News*—"Yesterday afternoon a young man who was enjoying a skate on Kent's Pond fell through the ice and received a rather cold and uncomfortable bath."

In 1892 in St. John's, the "attention of the public" was solicited via Letter to the Editor of the *Telegram* under the title, "Christmas Crib," which the nuns of Belvedere had constructed and had on display at the orphanage. The letter explained that the traditional figures of the shepherds, kings, and the holy family had been "purchased from Paris at considerable expense" and were of "rare artistic skill." The writer followed up by noting the public was invited to come and "lay their gifts like the Magi at the feet of the infant Saviour" during the days following Christmas.

From the *Evening Times* of December 26, 1895: "The good old Xmas custom of carol singing is evidently gaining favour in the community; for Xmas Eve, the choir of St. Thomas's sang carols in the church and after service, and the C of E [Church of England] Cathedral choir visited the residences of several of the prominent members of the church." The paper also noted, "Last night after service, the Choir of the Mission church of Springdale Street visited the Poor Asylum and sang in several parts of the West End."

Several St. John's churches held musical events in the post-Christmas period and provided a good reason to venture out from the comfort of the fireplace. Sometimes editorial comment followed these events. One example is of the Methodist Sunday school concert of St. Stephen's Day (December 26) in 1889, which was described glowingly, saying "The anthems were well rendered," and "the sextet by young ladies of the school was a pretty piece," and "many encores were called for" (*Daily Examiner*, December 27, 1889). Audiences would expect nothing less, as the community's singers were high calibre. For example, the first time Handel's *Messiah* was performed in Newfoundland seems to have been on December 29, 1884, when the St. John's Choral Society presented the work under the direction of Mr. Handcock at the Athenaeum. The *Evening Telegram* commented: "It is indeed something to be proud of that our people have made such advances in musical art as to be able to produce this sublime composition."

These, then, were some outings St. Johners could make, along with the usual snow and ice activities that cold weather permitted.

CHRISTMAS and the SEA

There is no place in Atlantic Canada that is so far from the sea that the ocean would not have some influence on Christmas. There would be sons far from home on fishing schooners or serving as seaman aboard barques and brigantines that families on shore would be thinking about come Christmastime. Their daughters, too, sometimes sought adventure serving on various vessels, and they would be wondering if they were going to make it home for the seasonal celebrations.

Though it provided employment and adventure, serving on a sea-going vessel was not easy. Judith Fingard's book *Jack in Port* reflects on the sailor's life in Atlantic ports, and cuts through the romanticism: "The vicissitudes of a sailor's life included shipwrecks, murder on the high seas, and the ravages of disease." She further notes that even in port, the sailor was not free of the scourge of bad food, ill-tempered captains, cold and cramped quarters, vermin, and unsafe working conditions. So it would be little wonder a sailor would look forward to a visit home at Christmas.

Even those on land had connections to the sea. There were those building ships, and those who cut the lumber and dressed it so the ships could be built. There were government officials, insurance men, merchants, saloonkeepers, and victuallers, all with their own interest in the ships coming and going with the tides. Seafarer's Mission personnel would also be watching, and standing ready to do their acts of kindness, especially as the Yuletide approached. In this chapter, we look at all sorts of activities that can be said to have had a connection with the people, the Christmas season, and the sea.

Saint John was the leading builder of wooden ships in the Atlantic area between the 1850s and 1880s. Shipyards and lumber mills lined the shores of the community, as the latter had to provide the raw material for the ships to be built and the cargoes of lumber that those newly built ships would carry to England for sale. It was always hoped the new ship would be sold along with its cargo, as that proved most financially rewarding to the owners of the ship.

Lumber milling and shipbuilding were seasonal activities, of course, so one might imagine that not much work would happen during the festive season, but on at least one occasion in Saint John, this was not the case. On December 24, 1879, at the mill of Hayford and Stetson in Carleton, which is now known as Saint John West, was the site of "one of the most pleasing events in connection with the festive season." The original report was from a Saint John newspaper, and was reprinted on December 20, 1988, by Don Smith, in his "Memories" column for the *King's County Record*. It had been brought to his attention by one of his readers, Mrs. John R. MacFarlane of Rothesay, who had sent him the old paper for his use and reproduction. It continued: "About 100 sat down to a sumptuous dinner prepared for them by the proprietors of the mill. The upper storey of the large new dry shed had been cleared out and a table erected extending the full length of the building. At one side of the room, a large circular table had been built for the occasion upon which the carving was done." The meal was described as having "no elaborate bills," but rather a "superabundance of good wholesome eatables…roast goose and turkey, baked pork, potatoes and vegetables…pies, tarts, pudding…and plenty of good tea and coffee," with everything "steaming hot."

The owners of the mill were not present, being with their families in Bangor, Maine, but as the article stated they "did not forget those who worked in their employ," and had staged the banquet to "strengthen the unity of feeling that is necessary between employees and employer for the successful operation of any works such as theirs."

"Such gatherings," the report noted, "are the exception, rather than the rule in our community." Indeed, no other banquet by the sea was found in any other area reviewed.

However, there were many reports of banquets just as lavish on ships of the era, both those berthed in ports and those out to sea.

The *Saint John Globe* gave a peek into one of these banquets in a report on December 23, 1888. The article was headlined, "Jack Tars Christmas," and pointed out that once the necessary work was done on-board a ship (for this could not be neglected for even an hour), after the ship had been "made safe and snug," Jack could think of having a treat of "bean soup and Christmas pudding." Sometimes, the report noted, a "kindhearted officer" would wish the sailor a merry Christmas and "slip him something to warm him up." When conditions permitted—usually when in port, or when the ship had just left port—"Christmas dinner is made as sumptuous as the paymaster's stores will permit." The *Saint John Globe* report also noted: "Sometimes there would be greenery and colorful bunting decorating the mess, and if there was a musician aboard, Jack would be piped to dinner." It continued: "On Christmas Day the sailors would be given an opportunity to overhaul their clothing, write letters and smoke outside the daily regulation hours." If the vessel was in port, the Christmas dinner was more sumptuous, as it was possible to get fresh fruit, vegetables, and meat. Sometimes, upon completion of the meal, the sailors would be given shore leave.

There are many accounts, primarily from sailors' diaries, that reflect on Christmas Day at sea. In *Courage Below and White Wings Above*, author Francis W. Grant had access to a notebook kept by Danny Gerrard of Malagash, Nova Scotia, who spent Christmas 1883 on the vessel *Blythswood*, sailing between London and Calcutta. It was not a pleasant voyage, and Gerrard stated his hunger was never satisfied the whole round trip. This included Christmas Day, even though the captain let it be known he "always gave his crew a first class Christmas dinner." However, the crew noted there was "little preparation for the meal taking place," as they went about their duties as noted above. When suppertime came, there were "two very small, thin chickens" to be "divided among sixteen hungry—almost starving—men," with gravy that was "little more than water." The plum

This card would seem appropriate as a Christmas greeting from a sailor at sea, though there is nothing inscribed to indicate that was the case in this instance.

pudding was dubbed "railway plum pudding," as the crew said it had "one raisin at each station." The captain sent a bottle of rum to the meal, but such a small bottle that the men would have gotten "a tablespoon each but did not even take that; they sent the bottle back to the captain, saying they were 'total abstainers.'"

The Yarmouth County Museum and Historical Research Library on the south shore of Nova Scotia has a large collection of documents that reference Christmas at sea. One of the most interesting is the account of Grace Ladd, a captain's wife, who was on-board the barque *Belmont*. Her account was written on December 31, 1894, while the ship was just off the south shore of Arabia.

With a crew described as "most miserable," and dealing with weather "very bad ever since we crossed the Gulf Stream," Grace wrote to her Papa saying, "Shanghai looks a long way off tonight." She told how "Christmas Eve Santa Claus paid us a visit," using the wig and beard she had kept from a previous Santa visit at sea, and "Forrest [her son] thought it was the same old fellow," and was "very much excited."

As far as food, another of her letters mentions "our turkey was delicious," and there was also a "ham boiled vegetable marrow...nice potatoes...a pudding...wine jelly nuts, etc. Pretty much what would be enjoyed in any landlubber's home anywhere."

Another letter that survived the long voyages of the era was from Nova Scotian Alice Wetmore, aboard the barque *Mary A. Low*, in 1902. Her December 25 entry reads: "Christmas Day was very hot. We had our stockings, which were filled with nuts, candy and oranges, the same as at home. After breakfast we opened our presents...everyone on board had a dinner of turkey, plum pudding, and mince pie." The entry concluded: "It was a nice Christmas, but not much like we had at home."

On Prince Edward Island, there was sometimes concern about how the sea would affect Christmas travel. Although our concerns with holiday travel mostly concern road conditions today since the Confederation Bridge links the Island to the mainland, in the 1880s, ferry service was the only way to and from PEI, and was only available until the ice froze solid in the Northumberland Strait. The date of the big freeze was, of course, unpredictable, and sometimes resulted in the ferry being taken off its run prematurely, as the December 24, 1888, *Daily Examiner* noted. "The merchants of Charlottetown are greatly annoyed on account of the report that *Stanley* [the ferry] is now to be taken from this route. The harbour is open; the weather soft...and large quantities of freight have been collected here."

In such conditions there were inevitably those who took chances on the strength of the ice and lost the gamble. Such is a case reported in the *Charlottetown Patriot* of December 22, 1893, which read: "On Tuesday forenoon last, while Mr. John Henderson of Bedeque was crossing the ice to Summerside with a carcass of pork and a tub of butter on the sleigh, the horse broke through the ice at McDonald's Point. Another horse and wagon came to the rescue, and the horse, and twelve men were placed on the rescue wagon, which then broke though the ice and the poor animal pulling the wagon drowned." Such incidents were not uncommon in the period of freezing up, which often coincided with the festive season.

The iceboats over the strait were certainly an unusual sea-connected feature of the season on the Island. In 1885, a report in the *Summerside Journal* described six new boats under construction by Robert Campbell. The cost of the boats was to be $100 each, and they were to be so much lighter than former boats, that it would only take four men instead of six to pull them across the ice and slush, or pass open water in the Northumberland Strait. The boats did not always accomplish the task without mishaps, sometimes becoming stranded or blown far off course by drifting ice, but there were few losses of life. If someone wanted to get home for the Christmas season and the ferry service was suspended, the boats were, at times, the only way. That is, until 1917, when ice-breaking ferry service was provided by the steam vessel *Prince Edward Island*.

No sector of what is now Atlantic Canada paid more attention to the sea in December than the residents of Newfoundland. Almost every commodity needed for the successful celebration of the Christmas season had to be delivered to the island by sea-going vessels. Hardly a day in December passed that publications such as the *Evening Telegram*, the *Carbonear Herald*, or the *Western Star* did not contain news of vessels' arrivals and state the type of "seasonal goods" they carried. Such was the case in the *Telegram* of December 24, 1883, which noted the "S.S. *Coban*, Captain Anderson, arrived from Boston at 8 o'clock last evening," and "Captain Hurst from New York via Halifax put in an appearance about 11 the same night."

The same paper's 1881 Christmas edition gave an extensive list of cargoes these ships carried, noting the SS *Bahama* brought "Canadian turkeys, geese, and fowls in prime order...eggs, choice cabbage, 'winter keeping' apples, parsnips, carrots, beets by the barrel, dried sage and savory and all sorts of pig delicacies, such as pork, jowls, hocks and tongues." Other vessels in the "foreign-going trade," were reported to have brought "Spanish, Portuguese, and Italian wines...Scotch whiskey and West Indies Rum," adding, "there was no shortage of the 'cup of cheer' or the novelties for children of every household."

However, not all went according to plan with every voyage; there were often instances when ships did not reach their destinations. One was reported December 24, 1880, under the headline "Loss of the Royal Arch," describing a schooner belonging to the Alward Brothers which had been bringing a load of potatoes, turnip, beef, and poultry to St. John's. It had been driven aground and wrecked on Green Island while making for Bay Bulls. There were, thankfully, no lives lost in this instance.

In the St. John's *Evening Telegram* of December 24, 1889, an anonymous Newfoundlander provided an account that begins, "As the festive season is now fast approaching, some of your readers might like to have an account of how Christmas is spent elsewhere. It was in the year 1884 that I took passage on the good ship *Hurunni*." The account continued, explaining the voyage through the West Indies in the Caribbean, and the ship was within "two or three degrees of the line [equator]" as Christmas approached, and actually crossed it on Christmas Day. This seems to have called for a celebration, and the account notes it began with "all hands on deck" where the "captain led the service," and "all things considered, gave us a very good sermon." This was followed by the sound of the dinner gong, and "we sat down to a repast fit for a prince of the blood. One might well have imagined he was dining in merry England." Dinner was followed by toast to "the Queen, the army, the navy, merry England, etc.," and then the writer noted, "We adjourned to the deck, where, under snow-white awnings, we enjoyed our cigars."

Certainly one of the most unusual Christmas-connected cargoes to arrive in Newfoundland occurred at the Bay of Islands in January 1908, when the steamer *Anita* arrived carrying three hundred reindeer. They were intended for St. Anthony where they were expected to "pasture beneath the snows" on the hillsides surrounding the famed hospital of Dr. Grenfell. The reindeer were said to be in "excellent condition," despite "ice and gales" and had not exhausted the "moss necessary for their sustenance," which had been carried in the hold of the *Anita*. Though the experiment seemed a success during Grenfell's lifetime, the animals had been carrying a parasite that eventually got into the native caribou through interbreeding. This led to a slew of problems that were not anticipated on that post-Christmas delivery of 1908.

When ships arrived at Christmas and during the winter season, it was often after much delay due to storm conditions, low provisions, or the vessel being ice coated. Some sailors would have frostbite or were sick in other ways and were seeking relief from their various maladies, or just needed a break from the hard life at sea. They found it in the benevolence of many organizations that were formed in the late 1900s.

In New Brunswick, sick sailors would head for the Marine Hospital on Britain Street. This was New Brunswick's first hospital and was funded by a levy on every ship that berthed in the province. If the ship arrived at Christmastime, the sailor would find the hospital "nicely trimmed with spruce, and everything looking very clean," according to a *Saint John Globe* account of 1885. That year, the report noted, "Members of the Church of England Institute visited and delighted the hearts of the inmates by a liberal supply of good things to eat." After supper, "an interesting musical program was carried out." The following morning, Christmas Day, members of the Germain Street Baptist Church visited, sang for the sailors, and "gave each one a small parcel of refreshments in remembrance of the day."

While the norm was for seasonal visits and events to take place on Christmas Eve or Christmas Day, in 1907 the ladies of St. John's (Stone) Church entertained the sailors three days before Christmas at the Carleton Street Church. The *Globe* reported that the sailors had formed up at the Seaman's Mission on Prince William Street and marched two abreast to the Stone Church, a few blocks north, to enjoy the evening's entertainment, which, without doubt, would have included a good measure of scripture relevant to the Christmas season. What a comfort such programs must have been to the sea-weary sailors.

The MERCHANDISING of CHRISTMAS

One of the biggest complaints you hear about Christmas these days is the way businesses and corporations have monopolized and merchandized the celebration.

They, of course, are not the first to have done this.

In England, the Puritans banned Christmas in 1644 due to its associated boisterous and drunken activity. Oliver Cromwell's name is usually attached to this cancellation, but in fact it was the English Parliament, controlled by Puritans, who did the deed. Later, in 1653, Cromwell *did* become Lord Protector of England, and did feel strongly that Christmas was so debased from its religious roots that it ought not to be marked. However, *World Encyclopedia of Christmas* author Gerry Bowler says it is incorrect to solely link Cromwell's name with what was essentially the whole parliament banning Christmas—a ban that lasted until 1660.

When the Puritans arrived in America in 1620, they also outlawed Christmas in New England, and this lasted much longer than it did in

England; in fact, it was still banned in Boston as late as 1856. However, by then, most non-Puritans were marking Christmas as the social and family event of the year. Likewise, Santa was beginning to be established as the gift giver, developing from the time of Washington Irving's accounts in the early years of the nineteenth century till the 1860s.

At that time most people still did not hang a stocking or erect a tree. However, just after the middle of the nineteenth century, more and more people began to do both, and each year it became more popular.

Naturally, the merchants of the various cities and towns were happy to help fill those stockings and place gifts under the trees, and to have Santa's assistance to do this. As early as 1865, there are reports of Santa being present in a shop in St. Stephen, New Brunswick, where it was advertised that he would hold a levee in Beckett's Confectionery shop. There is no editorial follow-up that would prove the old gent was actually in the shop. Likewise there is nothing to indicate how successful this advertisement was. However, it can be assumed it worked in that location, as for the next thirty years, similar ads appeared for other stores. Although, as with the St. Stephen instance, there is nothing to prove a costumed Santa was ever actually present.

Three additional samples of this will prove this point. In Halifax, the *Daily Reporter* of December 18, 1872, ran an ad under the bold title "SANTA CLAUS," which is followed by a long list of fancy goods, pictures, toys, and stationery to be found at a store on Duke Street. The implication is that Santa himself has left the goodies there for shoppers to select.

It is 1883 before Newfoundland merchants get in on the act, but when they do, it is in a big way. On December 18, the *Evening Telegram* has a front-page promotion for Edward Smith and Company. It reads: "WELCOME ARRIVAL per steamship Hibernian. OLD FATHER CHRISTMAS has just arrived by above steamer and has brought such a variety of good things, funny things, and useful things, and no Christmas Evening party will be complete without some of the old Gentleman's Luggage."

"NEW BOOKSTORE–SANTA CLAUS' HEADQUARTERS," read a bold page-one ad in the *Summerside Journal* of December 11, 1884. The copy continued, noting, "REPORT has it that SANTA CLAUS is going to make the new bookstore his headquarters for the season, which is quite possible. The people of Prince County will please make a note of this as it will be to their advantage." Of course, the idea was that the public would flock to J. A. Ramsay's new store, which was conveniently located opposite R. T. Holman's, for the "Christmas cards and fancy goods," as well as books on every conceivable topic. Did Santa show up, or did it just remain a tantalizing possibility? This remains unknown, but is seems unlikely that a small merchant could bear the cost of a costumed Santa for the dozen days before the twenty-fourth.

Other PEI merchants alluded to a Santa experience with headlines like "HARD TO BEAT Old Reliable SANTA CLAUS" in an ad for Stentiford's seasonal Christmas store. "The Old Original and only Santa Claus has made his headquarters at Morris' Book Store" is another example.

Editorial comments sometimes worked Santa into their columns that basically supported their advertisers, too. One example is found in a description of Ramsay's bookstore in 1887, which stated: "Mr. Ramsay announces that Santa Claus has inspected his goods and pronounced them as just what the young folks want at this season." Again, it's unlikely Santa was found doing the inspection, but this did not remain the case. In Charlottetown on December 24, 1888, it was reported that in "Jas Patton and Co's shop, a real live Santa Claus was in the western window on Saturday." This is just one year after the first-ever store window appearance of Santa in Canada was staged in Saint John in the MRA's window in 1887.

Throughout the 1890s, appearances of Santa became more common in stores and at community events. Advertisers went beyond words, and began placing illustrations of Santa as part of their promotions. As Santa's image had not been standardized, the images still had the ability to catch the eye of the potential consumer. As time passed, larger stores began opening "toy lands," having Santa receive visits from children. This practice has continued to this day, though the stores who did it first are long gone.

Who were the leading merchants in the Atlantic area as Christmas was developing? How did they get into business and how did they grow their businesses? Where did they get their promotion ideas? What did they stock? Where did they get the merchandise? What were the prices like?

In the era we have been exploring, there were no national or international merchandisers in the Atlantic provinces, but each province had one or two firms that seemed to have stood head and shoulders above the rest. Without exception, they were locally owned, often by one individual. All started in their own small way, and grew to be leaders in their town or cities by virtue of hard work and a keen eye for the public's needs.

RT **HOLMAN** LTD
SUMMERSIDE, P.E.I
THE BIG MAIL ORDER HOUSE

Shopping From HOLMAN'S CATALOG is Safe and Satisfactory

HOLMAN'S CATALOG

R.T.Holman
SUMMERSIDE P.E.I.

Holman's Catalog Brings the Store to Your Door - -

You can do your shopping right in your own home when you have HOLMAN'S CATALOG—Order what you need and no more—without exposing yourself to the inclement weather and running the risk of contracting sickness.

Holman's Catalog brings this vast shopping place to your very door with its money-saving opportunities

It matters not whether you want Dry Goods, Furniture, Hardware, Crockery, Boots and Shoes, China, Silverware, Cut Glass, Groceries or all of these, Holman's can serve you best and save you money.

If you have received our Fall and Winter Catalog write for one immediately and secure your share of the rare values contained between the covers of this great book.

There are no risks—no uncertainties—positively no dissatisfaction when you shop from HOLMAN'S CATALOG, because Freight is paid to any railway station in Eastern Canada on cash orders amounting to $10.00 or over, when cash accompanies order.

R. T. Holman Limited
The Island's Biggest, Best and Busiest Store

An advertisement for R. T. Holman Ltd., from October 22, 1918.

Also a key to their success was that they were known for their quality goods, often locally produced, and fairness in dealing with the customers, who were guaranteed satisfaction or money cheerfully refunded.

On Prince Edward Island, it was the firm of Robert Tinson Holman of Summerside that fit this description best. There were others, but Holman was so adept at building his business between 1857 and his death in 1906 that he became known as "the Merchant Prince of Water Street." Holman had been born in Saint John in 1833 and as a young man had worked in a local dry goods store, before moving to Boston and working in a wholesale drugstore. He was known as a fastidious employee, with everything he was placed in charge of found to be in "perfect order and neatness," as one account of his life's work put it. This served him well as he grew his business in Summerside, which eventually expanded to Charlottetown. It was said there was no item for sale in the store he did not personally approve, and which he could not locate quickly for a customer. Christmas was, of course, the top season for sales. It seems a bit ironic that an atheist should do so well in a season celebrating the birth of Christ, but Holman was so successful that he was able to build Summerside's biggest store, three storeys high and stretching along Water Street for 134 feet. He also employed some sixty residents of the city. Surprisingly, he was not a big advertiser; the local newspaper in 1894 did not carry illustrated copy, as was the case with many of their competitors. Holman always claimed he could serve the customers so well because he kept in close touch with them. Most of them were farmers and came into Summerside from the country. He took pains to build relationships with these people, and always tried to have what they needed on hand. This brought them back to his store again and again.

The story of one of Nova Scotia's biggest family operations, the McCurdy family of Sydney, is much the same as Holman's. Founder of the business was H. H. McCurdy in 1869 in Antigonish. Upon his death in 1906, his tremendous success was attributed to his "sterling business qualities and sound judgment," according to author Claribel Gesner in a July 1969 article in the *Atlantic Advocate*, when the firm was celebrating its one hundredth year in Sydney.

The store had placed a huge double-page advertisement outlining the broad range of goods available for the anniversary sale. There was a "Fashion Floor" with coats, dresses, sportswear, and furs, "only the top grade of the very best furs"; the main floor had "shelves brimming with Canadian and imported merchandise from England, Scotland, and the Continent." There was even a china department, with goods selected from "world markets," and there were shoes, candy, cards, fabrics, draperies, and a paint department to help "select the correct colour to match those drapes, curtains, etc." In other words, most anything the householder could wish for. As one Sydney resident was quoted in the anniversary article: "If McCurdy's didn't have it, we didn't get it."

In Newfoundland, judging by the amount and size of advertisements in the 1880s and 1890s, the Ayre Store on Water Street in downtown St. John's would have been the place to shop. It was founded by an English immigrant, Charles E. Ayre, and had its beginnings around the same time as the others, 1859. Like the others, it was initially driven by the energy and business acumen of its founder, who also served as a politician from 1879 until his death in 1889. The business was continued by his one of his four sons, John (it is not clear what role the other three had in the business), who also served in the legislature while managing expansions of the business. Sadly, the Ayre Store went bankrupt in 1991 and is no longer a fixture of Christmas shopping in St. John's.

Our final look at the merchants who grew rapidly during the age that Christmas was developing differs from the examples given above. This Saint John store was not founded by one individual, but three friends who worked in retail. They were James Manchester, James Robertson, and Joseph Allison, who, on April 4, 1866, announced in the *Saint John Globe* they would be opening a dry goods business to bear their names, Manchester, Robertson and Allison, at 48 Prince William Street. It was their intention to keep a "well-assorted stock of fancy and staple dry goods." Within a few months, they found it necessary to expand their operation, and moved to Market Square. In 1875 they moved again to King Street, where the store expanded again and again, eventually comprising fifteen buildings and 200,000 square feet of space. The store continued to serve customers locally and across the county until it closed on December 31, 1973. Like the other successful merchants in the Atlantic area, the success of MRA's was attributed to their "strict attention to business and gentlemanly qualities," according to an 1875 Saint John business review.

When the store had its twenty-fifth anniversary at Christmas 1890, it, of course, focused on that milestone in its advertising campaign during the month of December. At that time, the company was not using much in the way of illustration, though their competitors were. The *Daily Telegraph*, in its review of merchant activity titled "Santa Claus in the shops," which gave glowing editorial endorsement to all the paper's advertisers, said this about MRA's: "They are now in the midst of their 25th Christmas sale. When Mr. Allison…was in the old country this season, he made a special effort to secure something novel in the fancy goods line which would possess the double merit of being pretty and cheap," and the writer pointed out, "how well he has succeeded." In other portions of the descriptions it was noted, "The different departments are crowded with eager shoppers from early morning till closing time, and the army of clerks are kept busy all day long." It was the writer's opinion that "few establishments in the city possess so many attractions."

In their 106 years of operation, the store, which advertised it was the "Maritimes' Leading Department Store," had many firsts to back up that boast. These included having the first electric light in Saint John, demonstrated in their show window in 1883, and the first appearance of a live Santa in their King Street window in 1887. In 1951, the firm sponsored eastern Canada's first Santa Claus Parade, and in 1967 they were

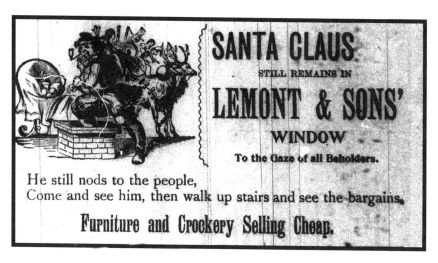

Lemont's promoted Santa at their Fredericton store in the Daily Gleaner *in 1894.*

the first department store in Canada to offer special shopping tours for senior citizens and people who were handicapped so they could do their Christmas shopping in comfort. For the last Christmas this program operated, MRA produced a flyer to guide the shoppers, and general manager Lloyd MacDonald wrote a message, which read: "We at MRA look forward to meeting you each year for this happy evening of Christmas music, refreshments, and browsing through the store...as in the past the friendly staff will be awaiting your visit, ready and willing to assist you." Information was then given on where the visitor could hear the carols sung, see Santa Claus, and enjoy complimentary holiday refreshments. All senior and handicapped visitors received a 10 percent discount on this evening, which was likely much appreciated. No one at that party had any idea it would be the last one (and in fact, on the last page of the flyer the company had asked for suggestions for future events).

The December 1911 issue of *The Busy East Magazine*—a publication that promoted merchandising and trade among the manufacturers and merchants of the east coast—used their editorial space that year to explain to its readers the "Economic Effect of Christmas Trade." The article began: "The various aspects of the Christmas rush of trades are worthy of more careful thought from the tradesman and businessman than they generally receive. Christmas, with its attendant festivities probably occasions more changing of money universally than any other one event." Though the article has no byline, any of the individuals mentioned in this section might well have penned those words based on the success they had with the Christmas trade in their various communities.

The chapter that follows gives more detail on what specific items people shopped for, and how it became increasingly popular to exchange gifts as part of the festive season.

TOYS, GIFTS, and GIFTING in the DAYS of OLD

~ⓄⓄⓄⓄⓄ~

The idea of exchanging gifts at Christmas is a very old one, as is evident from reading in Atlantic papers over the decades. In addition to the advertisements themselves, editors, anxious to get the advertising dollars, were liberal with promotion of the idea of gifting through their columns. Sometimes they offered advice, and sometimes employed humour, as can be seen in the examples that follow. Firstly, some of the earliest advertisements:

New Brunswick Courier January 16, 1847

Christmas Toys

The subscriber has just received per "Helen May" from New York:

A splendid assortment of German toys suitable for Christmas and New Year presents; which will be sold at very reduced prices at his store a few doors below the Saint John Hotel.

December 19, 1846, William Warn.

JANUARY 19, 1863
Fancy Bazaar
26 King Street, Saint John

Toys, Portmonaies [literally: money holders, wallets], Reticules [hand-bags], Dressing Cases and a Multitude of Novelties. A. Page offers his thanks to the public for past patronage, and [has] taken the earliest opportunity to advertise his new stock of English, French, and German TOYS, consisting of an infinite diversity of the latest designs, including 700 lbs. crystal and silicate beads, interesting games, laughable puzzles, choice rich and novel articles for girls and presents. His assortment of Ladies Companions, Reticules, Work Boxes, Dressing Cures, and elegantly scented hair oil he will offer at such unusually low prices that he feels confident of further favors from the public generally of St. John. These new and fancy goods have been personally selected by A. Page in the European Markets for cash, and he is determined to offer them at prices which shall defy competition. N.B.: Peddlers will find it to their advantage to call and examine this stock. Cheaper than ever.

The *Halifax Daily Reporter* of December 21, 1872, shows this growing custom was not confined to New Brunswick, as in this editorial:

This is the season for making your nearest and dearest relations, and to all other friends, presents. The custom is an old one, and to some a very good one. Pater Familias becomes sorely pressed about this time to find out what to give, and where to get it; and then if he should have a little regiment of nieces and nephews, and grand-children and god-children, (as very many of them have) why, his situation becomes more and more perplexing. The juvenile mind for the past week or more has been exercised with "Great Expectations" of Christmas and "Santa Claus"; and it is only right and proper for all those heads of families, in the position indicated above, and all others interested, to know where to go to make suitable purchases for the little folks and their friends. Mr. H. T. Hall, "Stationers Hall," Hesslein's Building, makes a gorgeous display of Christmas goods—everything in fact to please the taste and fancy of the most fastidious. Books rare and costly, set out in all the magnificence of calf, morocco and gold-comprising poetry, prose, history, biography, incidents of travel, fiction, etc., are to be seen in all the various styles of binding. Numerous little nic-nacks, such as please and interest the young folks are displayed in profusion. The show made by Mr. Hall is really unique, and it is *a study in itself; and then, to add to the charm of the surroundings, beautiful flowers, fresh from the Horticultural Gardens, are tastefully arranged about the show-windows and book-shelves, forming a pretty kaleidoscopic picture, which is not the least attractive feature of the display of holiday goods. All those who are generous (and those who are not ought to be at this season) and are disposed to make presents to their friends and relations, should visit Mr. Hall's store where we feel confident they can be suited to a T."*

HALIFAX MORNING CHRONICLE DECEMBER 19, 1888
C. J. Cooke and Son's store is, as usual, the children's paradise. It is full to overflowing of everything conceivable to make young hearts happy, and–in the case of horns and drums–old heads ache. When examining the wonderful stock of toys exhibited in this store, I could not help regretting that the date of my birth had not been postponed. I won't say how many years, until the present year of grace, 1888, because the toys provided for the rising generation are so much more pretty and ingeniously contrived; also, they are so much cheaper than when I was a small child. I was perfectly bewildered by the profusion of dolls, games, mechanical toys and numberless other pretty and amusing things piled up in every direction–dolls that went to sleep without paregoric, and on waking up called, "mamma" in a pretty little voice, instead of rending the air with piercing screams like some of their little human sisters; carts that were musical; sleds, tricycles, tops, and an endless variety of other things which will no doubt bring sunshine, and perhaps some noise, into many happy city and country homes. By all means, "old folks" go to Cooke's if you want to fill the stocking of your "young folks" and make them happy on Christmas morning.

Outside of Halifax, the business of giving was just as important. The *Yarmouth Light* of December 22, 1892, championed the "joy of giving," and noted how, "we find ourselves interested in many other people," and that "our hearts are melted and made liberal to others." Of course, this had a positive aspect too, as can be seen at the other end of the province, where the *Sydney Post* commented on the "busy times," at Christmas in 1901, and how the "Christmas trade [is] now moving at its height, and freight has been rolling in in large quantities," necessitating, "the importation of a small army of truck men," and that "nearly all the stores have employed additional help," and that the post office men had "rolled up their sleeves" and were busy handling packages of "all sizes and descriptions until all hours of the night," conveying "gifts to and from all parts of the country."

As part of their pre- and post-Christmas news of the communities, the papers often did interviews with seniors who could comment on Christmases of the past. Such interviews often provided background information on the toys and shopping of yesteryear, such as this one titled "Christmas Half a Century Ago," which was found in the *Saint John Daily Telegraph* of December 19, 1905. (Thus, the date referred to in the story paraphrased below would be 1855.)

This article is a reminiscence of the "good old days," when "mother and grandmother, stylishly arrayed in finery," would go Christmas shopping. It points out this was an era "of old-fashioned winters with their mountainous snow banks," when the "merry tinkle of sleigh bells" would not have been interrupted by the "screech of trolley…[or]…the rumble of electric cars." Shoppers would find stores in the "gayest Yuletide garb," but what they would not find was the diversity of gifts that were available in 1905, or as the author put it, there was "a limited assortment of fantastic creations…a toy here and there, and some high-class staples," and that "St. Nicholas had to pay considerably more for his goods," than was the case in the present age. As an example, the writer describes a "rudely made doll of wax and wood," then sold for two dollars but was just twenty-five cents at the time of writing. It continued, noting, "Bellows toys such as quacking ducks, squawking parrots, chirping birds, and barking dogs were among the leaders, and roughly made." Also popular were Noah's

Sumner's of Moncton offers their gift suggestions in 1923.

Evening Telegram, *December 17, 1896.*

Arks, "(which pre-dated the 60s by a considerable number of years)" and in the Ark's interior, "stuffed with brown paper and excelsior," where there were to be found "miniature cows, cats, and elephants." There were a "few mechanical toy and clock work goods," but by reason of their "exceptionally high price, remained only for those children born with the proverbial silver spoon in their mouths." The article also described the reading matter available for gifting, noting there were none of the popular annuals of 1905, such as Chums, Boy's Own and Girl's Own, but popular then were works by "Ballantyne [R. M. Ballantyne; Scottish writer and artist famous for his juvenile fiction] and Captain Marrya [Frederick Marrya, a British naval officer known for his sea stories]." Their popular works sold at a dollar per copy, and could be purchased a half century later for half of that or less. The final comment was on candy, noting that a half-century earlier, there was "no cream or caramel candy or chocolate confectionery," but only hard candy—and even that was expensive at twenty-five cents per pound.

There is another reminiscence of this period from Saint John *Progress* of December 22, 1894, which again looks back to the earlier period when merchants began to promote gifting.

"Most of the Christmas presents of my boyhood days," says a clever writer, "were designed by the manufacturers for the hanging stocking. Any too big to go into a stocking had to go over to somebody's birthday. In any family where there was more than one child, the older reliable "Noah's Ark" was always looked for. We hailed it with acclamation. Of astonished recognition, Noah and Mrs. Noah, Messieurs and Mesdames Shem, Ham and Japheth. There was no way of telling the men and women apart; they were exactly alike; but the elephant and giraffe you could distinguish at a glance, on account of the spots on the giraffe. So also the dog and the cow; because the cow was always white and blue, while the dog was invariably plain blue. Within twenty-four hours after landing on Ararat, the baby would have all the paint sucked off of Shem. Ham and the hired man and the doctor would be sent for. He told us, once a year, returning with the breathless messenger to keep the candy out of the baby's reach, and let it wean itself on the rest of the antediluvians if it found them to its liking. The red monkey climbing a red stick was another regular Christmas visitor. He was highly esteemed as a light luncheon by the baby.

It never seemed to effect this infant unpleasantly, to himself that is; although the cloudy symphony in red and blue about his innocent mouth was apt to make the beholder shiver. But it made the monkey look sick. Then there was a soldier on the box, with a major general uniform beating a drum. You turn a crank, the general lifted his sticks high in the air, and something in the box made a noise as much like a drum as a peal of thunder is like a piccolo. These things as toys were of no great value, but as practical and useful objects, lessons, they were beyond all price, on the minus side.

Christmas Toy Reports, 1878 and 1913

First, 1878: "Who ever saw in St. John such a display of Christmas Toys as are to be seen this year? It would seem that almost all the general stores had gone into the toy business in the hope that other branches of trade being dull, this one would be lively. [...] Peep into almost any window on the streets where a retail business is done and dolls may be seen of every kind and sort. There are dolls with lovely faces, hair that can be combed, and fingers that being jointed will close, eyes that can be moved energetically, [...] dolls that can speak, and most charming of all, dolls that can cry."

EIGHT A. M.

They are quiet at first—both the girls and the boys.
Too happy to make any riot or noise,
And they mentally show to each other their toys.

SIX P. M.

But see! In the nursery a terrible racket!
The dolls lose their heads, there are rents in each jacket,
And if you've a toy it's the fashion to crack it.

A child's Christmas day in the Daily Telegraph *on December 24, 1894.*

There are dolls of "bisque, rubber, china, wood...variously dressed, and excellently behaved," especially, as the article pointed out, "for boy dolls."

Then, 1913: According to an article titled "Christmas Toys and Child Labour," many of the dolls—especially those representing woodland Brownies—were being pieced together as "cotton-batting creatures" in tenement houses in New York, where conditions were not sanitary. Thus those buying the dolls were vulnerable to various diseases that flourish in such "overcrowded and unwholesome dwellings."

Also in 1913, New York State passed regulations banning children younger than fourteen from working at these toyshops. It was thought dolls from European sources were made under more strict conditions, but an investigation revealed the same sort of child labour in the old world as was the case in the new.

Beginning in the 1880s, Eaton's catalogues heralded a major change

"Jolly games for little folk" in the December 17, 1921, issue of the Saint John Globe.

in consumer purchasing. The first one came out in 1884, but there was no Christmas-specific catalogue until 1925. At first, the catalogue came from Toronto but later, catalogues were printed all over Canada. In Atlantic Canada, the catalogue came from Moncton, New Brunswick, where Eaton's opened a huge catalogue office in February 1920, and sold goods specifically for eastern Canadians. As an example, the catalogue for 1901 listed the following:

> *Christmas annuals – Chums, Boy's Own and Girl's Own: $1.75*
> *Books – Uncle Tom's Cabin: $.85, Black Beauty: $.45*
> *Candies – Chocolates: $.40 pound, chocolate almonds: $.40 pound, rock candy: $.20 pound, cream mixture suitable for a Xmas tree: $.10 pound,*
> *Toys, Dolls and Games – Dolls: $.15 to $7.00, iron toys $.10 to $2.00, crokinole board: $.90, drums: $.25 to $1.00, tool chest: $.25 to $4.50, skates: ladies $1.45 and men's (hockey) $5.00, mouth organs: $.25 to $.75.*

Humour was used to some degree to poke fun at both the shoppers and those who would receive their purchases. This example, "A Lesson for Christmas," came from the *Carleton Sentinel* of December 25, 1903:

How a generous giver of presents may retaliate for neglect:

"Here's something cheap. Let's buy it," said the tall, angular woman.

"What for?" asked the jolly little one.

"Oh, for a Christmas present," answered the other.

"Who for?" queried No. 2.

"Oh, I don't know. It will come in handy for someone."

"Here" (to the clerk), "wrap me up two of these and hurry my change, please. How much? Seventeen cents? Oh, all right."

"My goodness!" ejaculated her jolly companion. "You don't mean to say you buy all your Christmas presents that way?"

"Pretty nearly—at least that's what I intend doing this year. I've taken a lot of pains to buy things before, but from now on I'm going to go about things differently."

"Why, what has changed you?"

"Well, it's this way: I'm an old maid, you know, but I like pretty things awfully well. I am accounted well off, and so I am, but almost every year I have sought out the nicest, prettiest things I could find and sent them off to those I count my friends. And what did I get in return? Nothing, positively nothing. Now, the value of a thing doesn't count one bit with me, but I do like people to be thoughtful, and when I get two or three marked down calendars and a general collection of stuff picked up to send at the last moment which is not of the least use to anybody I rebel. So this year, I am going to try to teach them a lesson."

Goodness explained and rewarded was a *Charlottetown Daily Examiner* editor's take on the growing custom of gift giving. The short poem he selected (author unknown but not likely local), demonstrates how a greedy girl does not get what she hopes for. No doubt it was a lesson intended for a few young ladies and perhaps inspiration for a few parents or young suitors, when it appeared on December 22, 1885:

There once was a girl
As sour as a churl
Save when she knew Christmas was coming;
And then she was good
And at her tasks, would
Go round in her happiness humming.

How kind to her pa
To her brother and ma!
How genial, loving and pleasant
She was to her beau!
She wanted, you know
From each a magnificent present.

They fathomed her scheme
One night in a dream,
And each gave a package marked 'Candy';
On top, sweets she found,
But shaking them round.
The bulk, she discovered, was sandy.

On the more serious side is this Charlottetown editorial called "Preparations for Christmas," which explained the impressive lengths local stores went to that year:

Preparations for Christmas in the stores of Charlottetown have this year been made on an exceeding extensive scale. It is safe to say that never before did the mercantile establishments of this city make such elaborate displays as in the present Christmas time.

One need only walk the business streets and glance at the stores on either side to become fascinated or charmed with the panoramic views…compared to town of its size the merchants of Charlottetown will surely hold a foremost position in the selection and arranging of stock and introducing, to the public in the most presentable way, their varied and special lines. It is not unusual during these evenings to see crowds gathered about the store windows viewing the magnificent displays, and watching the movement of mechanical animals and various articles in natural motion…the public will enjoy every facility in making selections for Christmas in their very own city.

This is an edited version of what shoppers experienced in Charlottetown as reported in the *Guardian* of December 24, 1898. (Note: while December 24 may seem late for such an article to appear, it has to be remembered that stores stayed open very late on Christmas Eve, as they did not operate from 9 A.M. to 9 P.M. as malls do today. Advertisers also promoted gift giving in a more personal manner than is found in promotions today.

One example (of hundreds) that illustrates this was in the *Charlottetown Guardian* in December 1894. A young girl in a nightdress was sketched in the first of three panels, saying:

Please Santa Claus bring me:
a pretty dress
a nice warm fur collar
a fur cap and little muff
a pair of warm mittens
a pink pinafore
a pink wool scarf,
and, Dear Santa, I saw lots of other things I'd just love to have and they are
all down at Beer Bros.

This was followed by a second panel in the half-page of advertising that was titled "Sure to Please Your Wife," wherein Beer Bros. boasted they were "The Leading Fur Store on P.E. Island," and that "all ladies dearly love good furs."

The third panel featured a sketch of a young lady named Lizzie, who appeared to be of marriageable age and posed in a hat that looked like it was topped with grapes and eucalyptus leaves. She wrote to her friend Dolly: "I hope mamma will give me one of those pretty hats I saw in the Beer Bros.' store. Tom told me he was going to give me a lovely fur muff and collar and that is just what I want."

Whatever the weather, we'll weather the weather, whether we like it or not!

Weather affected shopping in times past just as it does today, probably to a greater degree as travel was more difficult in the horse and buggy age, and there were no bright and warm malls to wander as shopping took place. What conditions were like in the 1890s can be seen from this short report from the *Charlottetown Daily Patriot* of December 23, 1893:

The weather is very seasonable for the festive period, although if anything, it is somewhat on the cold side. Still, with splendid sleighing and plenty of wraps, those whose business or pleasure takes them abroad, appear to thoroughly enjoy it. Preparations for the celebration of Christmas Day and week are being pushed with all the old time vim. Daily the streets are filled with eager shoppers, while the merchants whose stores present very pretty appearances, report business as rushing. In the homes, all is bustle, and the air of expectancy familiar to Christmas pervades the household. In short, everything points to a joyous merry-making and determination on the part of all to remember that Christmas comes but once a year, and when it comes it brings good cheer.

Accounts of Christmas celebrations being cancelled are only occasionally reported in the papers of the late nineteenth or early twentieth centuries. Not that there were not storms or severe cold, but it would seem our ancestors took winter pretty much in stride. If they could not travel by wheel, they converted wagons to sleighs, bundled up, and went about their Christmas celebrations as best they could.

However, it is clear from the occasional news report that there were some disruptions to both pre- and post-season celebrations. On Prince Edward Island in 1911, the *Charlottetown Guardian* noted on December 26, "Saturday, the usual brisk trade among the merchants was greatly interfered with by a severe wind and rain storm. This lasted during the morning and afternoon…rain at times fell almost in torrents. Toward evening, however, an opportunity was afforded purchasers to get out and it was taken full advantage of."

In Newfoundland, in the year 1919, the *St. John's Daily News* of December 27 described a Christmas when people were pretty much forced to stay home following Christmas Day: "A North East gale, accompanied by snow…completely tying up all train traffic…snow drifts ten to twenty feet high…in the city, conditions equally as bad…snow drifts are piled almost to the house tops in places…suburban roads are next to impassible…street car service was suspended…it is unlikely that the cars will be operating today."

This comment from the *Saint John Daily Sun* on December 24, 1887, nicely summed up what many felt about Christmas gifting, and it is as true now as it was then: "It is a mistake—and there are many who make it—to suppose that a gift alone makes a Christmas merry. People today will buy expensive articles that they can ill afford—buy them because they are 'ashamed to offer a trifle.' It not infrequently happens that both the donor and the recipient of Christmas gifts are made 'uncomfortable' by this fact." When it was written, shopping may have been different, but it was already as important to the merchants—and the area's economy—as it remains to this day.

CHRISTMAS
in the HOME

⟨⟨⟨○○○○⟩⟩⟩

Were you given a chance to reflect on the Christmases of your youth, you might find that most of what you recall would be very much the same as others of your age. Then again, there might be interesting differences you could pass along to others so they could consider adding them to their celebrations of the season. This is why it is so good for writers to interview those who can comment on the past, and that is what we have been able to do in what follows so you can compare your own Christmas memories to four others from across the Atlantic provinces.

Looking back fifty years from 1906, an unnamed scribe in the *Saint John Daily Telegraph* noted: "Gift buying is easier than it was." Of the 1860s, the writer noted there was "no choice of toys," and "shops contained no wealth of novelties." There was only a "sprinkling of notions," such as "a toy here and there," and "St. Nicholas had to pay considerably more for his goods" than was the case in 1906. The writer then went on to describe the "rudely made dolls" and "bellows toys" discussed in the previous chapter.

"Then, Julia, let me woo thee—"

Holiday entertainers.

Where did these toys come from? A study of newspapers of the era clearly shows that most Saint John merchants made buying trips to England, and shipped the goods home. When the vessel arrived, its cargo would be listed in the papers of the day, and the public advised that no further shipments were expected, and they should buy immediately to avoid disappointment. These advertisements often continued to be seen in the papers for weeks following the festive season. There was no need for Boxing Day sales, or after-Christmas markdowns, it would seem, as the advertisements usually stated that prices were low to begin with.

Besides the mercantile concerns of the city, barbers also often offered toys as a sideline in this time period, which seems a strange mix; just why and how this came about remains a mystery.

To place this commentary in context, we are fortunate to have found a 1923 interview in the *Saint John Daily Telegraph* with an unnamed Rothesay woman who was able to look back seventy-five years and comment on the Christmases of her youth in Saint John. She mentions only one toy, recalling that her eldest brother and sister awoke early on Christmas morning, and were out on the "hard-frozen road at 5 A.M., trundling along on their velocipedes, which had been brought by Santa." Her comment is proof positive that Santa was a known gift-giver in this era, long before he was seen in the flesh by any Saint John child.

This lady remembered living in what she described as a big house, and though it had "large fireplaces," it also had "none too well heated rooms" in what was then referred to as Portland, and is now known as north-end Saint John. "The parlour," she said, was "a sacred room, and was for Christmas Day only." She added it was where they "reveled at looking at stiff pictures, the wonderful album and studying the strange things that were brought from far off lands by sea captains, friends of the grown ups."

She recalled the children were kept busy in the making of the pudding, but with a giggle told how a "good share of the raisins went into her mouth." The children were allowed to watch the pudding steam, as it was "hung on the crane in the big open fire." They were also engaged in turning the goose on the spit in the fireplace, until, "we were ordered out of the kitchen lest we got burned."

Another comment this Rothesay woman made proves the practice of hanging stockings by the fireplace—as in Moore's 1822 poem—was an early tradition in New Brunswick. On Christmas morning she recalled: "On tiptoe we ventured to the fireplace, about five or even earlier…the big fire was out [and] there was dim shadow everywhere. We had no doubt in those times that Santa had come down, pack and all, to give us of his store. It was a beautiful big chimney and no reasonable person of five or six or even ten, would be so slighting of tradition to think any other way." What appeared in those stockings on Christmas morning? She said, "I knew there would be money in the toe, but it gave me glorious thrill to find it, and then the nuts and raisins and an apple and a doll. I loved best of all the rag dolls." Candy she recalled was "that hard kind—what do they call it? Oh, yes, rock candy." At that point in the interview, the woman became very quiet, and the interviewer noted, "It became difficult to retrace our steps to the long ago."

Fortunately, through the recollections about to follow, we can slip back in time ourselves, and be immersed in Christmas in an era when it was just starting to take on the commercial overtones of the present day.

Carol McLeod's article "A Child's Christmas in Victorian Halifax," published in the *Atlantic Advocate* of December 1991, gives a glimpse of Christmas as it was in the 1880s from an interview she did with resident Emily Lee Johnson. Johnson recalled the children gathering around the unlit fireplace a few days before Christmas 1881, and when they heard a bell ring, they would stick their heads in the fireplace and shout up the flue to Santa, naming the gifts they would like to receive. This is certainly a unique family tradition.

A family gathers around a table with a HOLIDAY theme on the plates before the food arrives.

And what gifts did she and her five siblings receive? Even well into her nineties Johnson could still recall the "handmade mittens, handkerchiefs, store-bought dolls, tea sets," all "wrapped in white tissue paper" and either slipped into her stocking, or placed under the tree.

The diary of Sarah Clinch, edited by Meghan Hallett, also has an unusual and mostly forgotten custom. Clinch wrote on December 24, 1853: "The Christmas boxes were given out today as tomorrow is Sunday," and of course, no work was to be done on a Sunday in that time. On that Christmas her box contained "shoulder ribbon and belt…six pounds from Uncle Morton…a papeteur [paper maker] from Heber, and neck ribbon from Aunt Mary…a pretty little almanac." She enumerated what she gave as gifts as well, noting, "I gave Uncle William a book of blotting paper, Aunt Mary a bottle of lavender, Charlotte a bottle of mignonette, Louisa a papeteur like the one Heber gave me…Miriam some velvet bracelets, Heber Laurt's 'Essays of Life,' Bella and Tony collars, and the three boys neck ties."

On Prince Edward Island, what better source than Lucy Maud Montgomery's *Anne of Green Gables*, and the comments about Christmas? Montgomery lived from 1874 until 1942, so certainly she was in a position to have not only experienced the era when Christmas was developing, but, in writing her stories, to have talked to other Islanders who lived through the period. Though her work is fiction, what she wrote is likely a mixture of her own experiences and of the many stories she heard. Her Christmas scenes are true to what others through the region have related about Christmas in the latter part of the nineteenth century.

In *Anne of Windy Poplars*, Montgomery wrote: "The plum pudding was concocted" and the "Christmas tree brought home," describing it as a "beautiful little fir." She also wrote of "gathering spruce and ground pine for wreaths," and of how, at an "unearthly hour on Christmas morning, the family heard the ringing of an old cowbell up and down the stairs." While trees and plum pudding would have appeared in many Island homes, the cowbell incident is not found in any other readings consulted.

Like others who reflected on the era, Montgomery's description of the gifts Kathleen received shows us this was a simpler time, as she mentions receiving "a gay crocheted afghan, a sachet of orris roots, a paper knife, a basketful of tiny jars of jam and jelly, and a cheesy cat for a paperweight." *House of Dreams* has a description of Anne's first Christmas as a newly married woman. It does not go into detail about decorations or gifts, but does give a glimpse of the man's role in the celebration, as her husband, Gilbert, is charged with carving the goose for the first time. It adds, "Anne's first dinner was a great success," and "she beamed with housewifely pride." Though these events did not actually happen, they were likely based on Montgomery's own observations. She wrote that when the meal was over, "they gathered around the cheer of the red hearth flame and Captain Jim told them stories."

This is also true of Montgomery's descriptions of a Christmas in *Anne of Ingleside*. As everyone was gathered around "the lively tree, all gold and silver bubbles, all lighted with candles in the still dark room, with parcels of all colours, and tied with loveliest of ribbons…Santa appeared, a gorgeous Santa, all crimson and in white fur with a long beard and *such* a jolly big stomach." Her words draw us into PEI Christmases of yesteryear, and we can understand the joy and camaraderie Islanders felt, even though many decades have since passed.

Our final glimpse of home-style Christmas and the gifts and activities of the season comes from two sources found in the St. John's *Evening Telegram*.

The earliest comments appeared on December 23, 1891, under the simple title, "CHRISTMAS." Though the author of the piece is not identified, it's obvious he was not a native Newfoundlander when he wrote, "The strange land is home now," and how he enjoys "Christmas from all points of view in this new home-land of ours." In his discourse he asks, "Who is he who is unprepared to welcome it?" He then goes on to describe those elements most dear to him, saying, "Who would not miss Father Christmas, Christmas preparations, Christmas trees, Christmas fun and Christmas meetings, the holly, the mistletoe, the smiles, the Christmas dinner, the carols of joy and the sweet hymns of praise?" His list shows much of what we would miss today was already in place by 1891. He concluded, as we might even now, by stating, "Christmas is a delightful time. A Merry Christmas to you!"

The second is much later, December 22, 1955, and it's titled "Dreaming Back the Years: an Octogenarian sees Xmas." This title seems to indicate the memories gathered were from the 1880s, though some were incidents from the writer's mid-life, which would have been 1915 or so. At the outset of the story our octogenarian, who is never named, is reflecting on the children who have just been put to bed, and how it seems to her she was just a child herself. But, she notes, times were very different when she was twelve—in about 1883—and yes, very different from the Christmases her great great grandchildren would experience in the twenty-first century.

Her youth, she recalled, had been an era of "smelly oil lamps…no vacuum cleaners, no electric washers, no refrigerators, no stores to supply bread and ready-prepared or half-prepared foodstuffs, or soap and tea or sugar and salt in handy packets. All the sauces had to be homemade." The women, she said, should have been tired and miserable, grumbling, but she "did not remember any of them like that."

Christmas Day dinner, she said, was at three in the afternoon, and there would be fourteen around the table in "Gran'ma's house," which she recalled as "quite a squeeze" in the "big house that cost forty pounds a year to rent." She described the table, which had a "goose on one end, a turkey on the other, and there was a pickled beef and two great beef pies on the sideboard." She added, "There was plum pudding, mince pies, jellies

A typical Christmas tree of the 1940s.

in tall glasses, almond custards in short glasses, lemon cheesecakes, tartlets, and sugary buns, all homemade." In addition, there were oranges, apples, almonds, and raisins. Choices for drinks included "light and dark ales, homemade parsnip wine, and homemade sloe gin."

After dinner, the children were wrapped in robes and a trip was made to the Ragged School, where the children took their previous year's Christmas toys and gifts of boots and stockings for the "poor little barefoot urchins and their equally ragged parents." This did not conclude the day, though; in the evening the "carols singers came, the waifs were brought in and given money and food, for mostly they, too, were poor and a little drab." As she reflected, the woman noted, "The whole day had been more religious in character than those in later Christmases." She spoke of grown-ups who had a "service on Christmas Eve, and all, except the very tiny ones, had gone to church on Christmas morning."

As far as outdoor pursuits went, she remembered outdoor games were not played "on Christmas Day, unless the weather was suitable for skating or sliding." In the strangest statement of all, she noted, "Golf was unthought-of of then."

Inside, children's playthings were described as "simpler, but the children were no less happy with them." The boy's toys, she noted, "were deadly as they included bows and arrows, toy pistols, swords, and lead soldiers." Surprisingly, she did not mention what girls received for play.

It was a long interview, and this unnamed Newfoundlander ended the session by saying, "Things had changed much," in her lifetime, which earlier in the interview she had described as a "long, interesting journey" that "seemed to have passed very quickly."

The interviewer, Colin Brooks, concluded by noting, "with a quiet smile" the woman slipped "into a placid, happy sleep," which seemed a fitting way for her to close off her Christmas Day memories.

❦The
CHRISTMAS NUMBERS
of ATLANTIC CANADA'S
NEWSPAPERS

One of the seasonal delights for newspaper readers across Canada was an idea that came from British newspapers and magazines, which almost all published what they called a "Christmas Number." Primary among the periodicals was the *Illustrated London News*, which, as has been noted, was circulated all through the Commonwealth and was largely responsible for the spread of the idea of erecting, decorating, and lighting a Christmas tree indoors. This periodical also commented on other topics in the chapters of this book, such as games played at Christmas, the sailor's Christmas, the first appearances of Santa Claus in department stores, the singing in churches and around the community, the foods special to the season, fashion, travel, theatrical presentations, outdoor pursuits, etc. While these were primarily as it happened in England, from time to time editors chose to feature Christmas in other places like France and Sweden close to home, and Canada and the United States further afield.

Newfoundland

Among Britain's colonies was Newfoundland—until 1949, when a referendum led to the province becoming part of Canada. During the long years between Confederation and the middle of the last century, Newfoundland's ties with England remained strong, and merchants depended on British goods for Christmas gifting much more than any other region in North America. Thus, it does not seem at all strange that the British custom of the "Christmas Number" should appear first in the Atlantic provinces in St. John's *Evening Telegram*. This occurred in 1879 the year the paper was founded by William J. Herder. Its first editor was A. A. Parsons, who continued to serve in that role until 1903, and in 1929 wrote a history of the first fifty years of the *Telegram*. He noted that critics at the time of the paper's launch said it was "impossible to make a daily evening paper... pay in St. John's." Lively from the first, it was circulating 3,500 copies daily after the first year, and only continued to grow. One of its most lavish issues was the Christmas Number. As Parsons recalled, the "holiday issue was a gem, the 'art preservative of all the arts,'" and was worked up "to the highest point of literary and pictorial excellence." It featured "the best native talent, and there were literary giants among us in those days." He described these esteemed authors contributing to the Christmas issue's columns, and said the "efforts of some of the best engravers of England and America were requested to meet the paper's ambitious requirements." He further explained that "the Christmas Number was not a money-making enterprise, nor was it ever intended to be. The main object of those chiefly interested in the venture was two- fold: (1) To make each number better than its predecessor and (2) to exhibit to the outside world the artistic and literary capabilities of the Colony in this particular direction."

The issue of December 24, 1880 (Christmas Number volume 11, issue number 298), was four pages long and sold for one cent. The editorial was a front-page, three-column-wide feature, and the editor noted that all "well regulated papers" should not "go to press without a word to say about 'the morrow.'" He then did just that saying, "Make way there, if you please, for the Right Honourable Father 'Christmas.'" The editor then describes Christmas as a time of "peace and goodwill," of "Festivity and Jocund Mirth," and mentions among its delights Christmas cards, presents and trees, mince pie, roast goose, plum pudding, holly and mistletoe, and that the season is a "good-humoured time, and with this feeling we wish to each and all a Happy Christmas."

This was followed by a poem, "Christmas Bells":

Sweetly chime the Christmas bells,
Echoing o'er the frozen ground,
Up the mountains, down the dells
Gladdening all by their sweet sound.
Hark! The merry Christmas bells!
Happy, peaceful Christmas bells!
Chiming, chiming
Sweetly chiming,
Echoing over hills and dells,
Happy, peaceful Christmas bells!

On page two of the Christmas Number, another editorial appeared. This one inviting readers to "keep Christmas with gladness and great joy," and then employing a second bit of whimsical poetry, which was certain to put a smile on the faces of all readers. It began: "Beneath a shady Tree they sat…celebrating the joy of kissing." In the next column appeared a third poem, "The Babe of Bethlehem." This was followed by "A Christmas Legend," being the tale of "the Russian peasantry, and of the old woman Bobouska," who was to Russians what Father Christmas was to Newfoundlanders. Though editor Parsons claimed the Christmas Number was not a moneymaker, there was certainly a fair share of advertising in the 1880 issue. This included Water Street merchants, such as J. A. Scott's promotion of clocks, jewellery, and "20,000 oleographs and stamped pictures, and 30,000 cigars." Acme Club Skates were available at J. H. Collis and Powring Bros, while a few pairs of American skates and some very handsome mechanical toys (along with sleds and tool boxes) were promoted by Duchemin's General store, who, like most merchants, noted the goods were "just received per the SS *Sardinian* from Liverpool."

Page three kept Newfoundlanders up-to-date with the news from Europe, as it heralded the death of celebrated author Mary Anne Cross (née Evans), who had used the penname George Eliot to write *Middlemarch*. It also delved into the loss of the schooner *Royal Arch*, inbound from Prince Edward Island with a cargo of produce. It included a column on the benevolent work of the St. Vincent De Paul Society, and gave details of Christmas and Sunday services of various St. John's churches. There was an interesting column on how America celebrated Christmas, pointing out the "glad fun and revelry takes on a different character when filtered though the American mind."

A genuine Newfoundlander's contribution takes up most of page four, in a lament titled "Thoughts on Christmas Day," written for the *Evening Telegram* and dated Christmas Eve 1880. The initials "D. S." are the only clue to the identity of the author, who was obviously not in a celebratory mood. In a sense it gives a more melancholy dimension to the season that has only become acknowledged in recent times, with songs like "Blue Christmas." Thus, the *Evening Telegram* was far ahead of the times; as the editor stated in his fiftieth anniversary review, in that age editors were looking for articles that were "piquant, sparkling contributions." D. S.'s poignant poem begins: "Christmas is with us, the day of all days," and has eleven verses that describe sadness at the passing of old and dear friends:

> *The old chair in the corner looks empty and sad—*
> *Ah! too well we know of the cause:*
> *The dear one that filled it has gone from the home—*
> *The home which her presence made glad.*

Prince Edward Island

The most consistent use of the term "Christmas Number" on Prince Edward Island was the (approximately) six-by-ten-inch *Prince Edward Island Magazine* published in Charlottetown by Archibald Irwin from Christmas 1899 until January 1905. It was not strictly a Christmas issue as was the case with Christmas Numbers in Newfoundland, but the Christmas issue always had poems and stories delving into folklore or of historic interest, and copy relevant to the season. The first of the Christmas Numbers was actually the tenth issue in Volume 1. For an example of one story from this issue, see chapter 14 on ghosts, and a summarization of a then-fifty-year-old story, "The Phantom Bell Ringer." This story makes a case for the fact that some mysterious bells being sounded at the "Auld Kirke" were connected with the sinking of the island ferry the *Fairy Queen* in October 1853.

There was one other occasion when a ghost tale was part of newspaper contents at Christmastime, that being in December 1901, when a play whose author is identified only as "NEMO" was included. NEMO opened the piece "The Ghost" with the notation that the "Centre of Stage was open to all performers, and all the parts were 'bit' parts, no star part.'" It was accompanied by a very nicely done illustration of the ghost passing through a graveyard by James Horne, who the author thanks at the close of the play.

Illustrations were used sparingly in publications at the time, as engravings were still expensive to produce. However, in the first few and last few pages of each Christmas Number, PEI's merchants used illustrations effectively to catch patrons' eyes. Mitchell's Bookstore, opposite Prowse's, headed up their full-page promotion with the words "Santa Claus, the bringer of Christmas Joys." Unlike many others, Mitchell's included an image of Santa laying his finger aside his nose (as he does in the famed "Night Before Christmas") and promising bookstore patrons would get "good value for his money" when buying "toys, games, dolls, etc." The promo further stated that Santa "could fill the pages of *PEI Magazine* telling of the different kinds," but he "doubted the editor would permit this." Said editor was constantly looking for advertisers to cover the costs of the publication, so it is hard to say just what might have been permitted.

Further details in this advertisement gave hints as to the type of toy a child might have enjoyed in 1901. They were described as having been "imported direct from the manufactures" and that Mitchell's would never sell "shabby goods imported from jobbers on the other side." Just what that meant is not pointed out, but the type of toys included "mechanical, roaming, and there were also stuffed dolls and work boxes." Pictures also showed a jack-in-the-box, and a board game as possible gifts, but strange as it might seem, Mitchell's Bookstore did not mention it had books for sale!

Progress *newspaper was known for its quality artistic reproductions in an era when few newspapers used such images. For the period it was top-notch, and depicts a family showing off their well-lit tree at Christmas 1895.*

In addition to Mitchell's, other advertisers for Christmas slippers were Alley and Co., and Hazard and Moore noted, "Ever since last April we have been getting ready for the holiday trade," Miller Bros promoted violins, banjos, guitars, and autoharps, with an illustration of a family gathered around the living room enjoying a musical evening." T. B. Riley showed a gent relaxing in a huge chair, his feet up on a nearby table enjoying his pipe, while A. D. Reddin noted they had "surprised themselves" with the "variety and elegance" of their perfume display.

Advertisers from out of province also took advantage of the wide circulation of the Christmas Numbers, of which there were four (1899, 1901, 1902, 1903), with the principal advertiser being Saint John's Manchester Robertson Allison, who eventually called the big store on King Street in the port city "The Maritimes' Greatest Department Store."

Glancing thorough the five Christmas Numbers in the *Prince Edward Island Magazine* certainly brings that era, and the gifts and activities of that era, to life.

ᴏNova Scotia

On Saturday, December 22, 1877, the *Halifax Reporter* advertised "Our Christmas Number" and promised that the following Monday the paper would "form an excellent Christmas memento to forward to friends at a distance, as well as furnish a budget of appropriate and interesting reading for the home circle during the holidays."

Earlier, you read the St. John's *Daily Telegram* claimed to be the first publisher of Christmas Numbers, but this 1877 paper proves that statement incorrect. It is likely the author did not know of the Nova Scotia effort three years before his when he wrote the comments above.

So what did the Halifax paper carry in the true first Christmas Number? In its pre-issue promotion, the *Reporter* promised seven original articles, namely: "Christmas Sunshine" by Revered Doctor Burns; "The Period and Place of the Nativity" by Revered Rob't Murray; "The Prose of Christmas" by George Johnson, Esquire; "The Miseries of Christmas" by Fitz Cochrane, Esquire; "Good Cheer" by Reverend Thomas Duncan; and "Christmas Eve" by Revered Doctor Hill. In addition, the promo promised a "budget of local news, and news by telegraph from all parts of the world." The paper delivered on the pieces, and also included the usual well wishes to readers and a huge number of advertisements from area merchants, which did not differ to any great degree from those noted in the PEI Christmas Numbers.

New Brunswick

In our look at Christmas Numbers, we have had two large city papers, a provincial magazine, and now turn to a thrice-weekly paper with a circulation of around five thousand in a smaller centre of New Brunswick. The centre is Chatham, incorporated as a town in 1896, and a sister town of Newcastle on the Miramichi River in northern New Brunswick. The year is 1912.

The *Gazette Christmas Number* was published in Chatham, New Brunswick, by Jordon and Brown from offices on the south bank of the river on Water Street. The editor listed the paper's phone number as "10," and included his home number as well (159): an unusual thing for an editor to do. But he did not likely receive many complaints, for the high standard of this Monday, Wednesday, Friday paper was very much evident in its Christmas Number. The front page had a very high-quality photo of a young lady demurely holding the hem of her dress as her pets look on. There is no hint that this is a Christmas scene, but it is certainly a heart-tugging pose she has taken. The photo however, is surrounded with seasonal images of evergreens and holly wreaths with candles on tridents on each side of the photo. The cover surely shows the potential purchaser that this is not the usual edition of the paper, but something worth buying to while away an hour or two as Christmas approaches.

Its appearance on shelves was actually early for a Christmas Number; they were usually published on the last Saturday before the 25, but also often on the 24, and this one is dated December 16. There would have been three more issues to come out before the big day—and in fact one on Christmas Day itself, which was common at the time. None, however, could hold a candle to the Christmas Number for detail about the festive season.

The 1912 issue opens with a "very old story as told to children." It contains three more crisp images similar to the front page. The story is about "year one, when there was no Christmas Day," and how the calendar is dated

APPETITE THOROUGHLY restored when Adams' **TUTTI FRUTTI is used.**
See that no imitation is palmed off on you.

Commercial advertisers did seasonal promotions to sell their products, as seen in this family gathering sponsored by Tutti Fruitti in December 1894 in the Fredericton Gleaner.

from the birth of Christ in that long-ago year. It is a clever retelling of the Gospel that would have been known all too well by children in an age before Christmas became so secular.

As was customary with Christmas Numbers, the editorial is themed to the season and titled, "A Little Talk with Gazette Readers," and takes the opportunity to suggest that readers searching for "suitable and useful gifts," that "this edition merits careful reading." Indeed, it contained suggestions from "Harry Rich's Style Store for Men and Boys," the "Gazette Stationery Department." A. McLennan, normally a carriage and sleigh manufacturer, was diversifying and asking readers, "Will there be a Berliner Gramophone in your home this Christmas?" J. D. Creaghan's clothing company had an image of Santa for children to study. For readers planning outings, ads noted that at the exhibition rink "skating was assured," and that Babineau's Alleys were open for "bowling and pool." Christmas dinner would be served at the City Restaurant, or a Christmas Day sleigh could be booked from W. J. Groat, and that due to low temperatures the night before, the ice bridge over the Miramichi River was open. One unusual aspect of the Groat livery business was that for those up with the times, there were "autos to hire."

One of the strangest features of the Chatham Christmas Number was a full page of "photos by Sallows" of "Summer Holiday Time in Canada." It was mostly beach scenes with children enjoying shoreline experiences; except for the fact it was in black and white, it was as well laid out and inviting as any glossy promotion of modern times.

The short story "The Economy of Timothy Allgood" by Frank L. Channon was the obligatory fiction all Christmas Numbers were expected to contain. Most editions were not as lavishly illustrated as was the case in the *Gazette*, which had five Dick Hartley drawings to bring the story to life. There is no mistaking the fact these were lifted from a paper from England, as in one of the cartoons the subtitle mentions the man working for a "bob a week."

Overall, this Christmas Number would not have to take second place to anything of this type that was being produced in the era noted.

Further Afield

"Good Christmas, whom our children love,
We love you too! Lift us above
Our cares, our fears, our small desires!
Open our hands and stir the fires
Of helpful fellowship within us,
And back to love and kindness win us."

This poetic sentiment was written by Edward Sanford Martin and appeared in the Montreal-based *Family Herald* on December 22, 1915. It is representative of the Christmas sentiment of the widely circulated weekly paper. As the nineteenth century closed and the twentieth century began, the *Family Herald* did more than any other Canadian publication in establishing uniformity in Christmas celebrations from coast to coast.

Of course, the Atlantic provinces were included in this; in fact, the *Herald* was probably the only paper that circulated in all four provinces, as the city dailies were, before the days of the internet, confined to their local distribution areas.

The *Family Herald* originated as the *Family Herald and Weekly Star* in 1869, and was founded by Hugh Graham, publisher of the *Montreal Star*. This was just two years after Confederation, but of course Prince Edward Island and Newfoundland–Labrador were not yet part of the Dominion. However, the paper likely circulated in both provinces, for it had wide appeal to agrarian communities, and its aim was to help those in rural areas "keep pace" with the advance of "scientific knowledge and practice" of farming. That the paper found favour with both urban and rural

Canadians is shown by the fact that in 1900 the company was able to erect a seven-storey office at 165–169 St. James Street in Montreal.

The content of the *Family Herald* included columns such as "Woman and Home" and carried "clean and wholesome" stories and sketches. There was a section on "Travel and Adventure," and one titled "Questions and Answers," where editors promised medical, scientific, and legal problems would be dealt with by a "specialist in that particular field."

Through December, the paper carried articles from contributors across Canada to help its readers celebrate a joyous Yuletide. There were food tips, entertaining ideas, how to's for decoration and gift giving, secular and sacred poems and prose from the world's best authors, sheet music to play, games to try, legend to wonder about, and images of Santa at a time when he was seldom seen and still a very mysterious personage.

When the *Herald* published a Christmas idea, chances were a boy on Cape Breton Island or girl in Newfoundland, or a mother or father in New Brunswick or Prince Edward Island would enjoy the same story, do the same craft, or see the same image of Santa. In homes across the region, "Jingle Bells" would be played as it was notated, games played as written, and seasonal foods prepared following the recipes given. Thus, it can be said that the *Family Herald* homogenized Christmas in the east, as it did across the county.

While it is known that many Canadian children did receive *St. Nicholas Magazine* (and other American publications), the chances of seeing a Canadian author or illustrator in these US magazines were slim. By contrast, the *Family Herald* regularly ran contests encouraging written and illustrated submissions from young Canadians. Over the years, many authors and illustrators from across the nation had their work published in the paper, including many who became well known, including several Atlantic Canadians. These included Lucy Maud Montgomery, *Chronicles of Avonlea*; Wilfred Grenfell, *Labrador Children Who Know No Santa Claus*; Evelyn Richardson; Thomas Raddall; and T. Goodridge Roberts to name just a few.

CHRISTMAS COULD HAVE BEEN CANCELLED in ATLANTIC CANADA

<del>~∽ᢒᢒᢒᢒᢒ~</del>

There is a popular misconception that it was Puritan Oliver Cromwell, later known as Lord Protector of England, who cancelled Christmas in the middle of the seventeenth century. In actual fact, Christmas in 1645 was cancelled by the English Parliament—a cancellation that lasted until 1660. No one knows how much of what constituted "old-time Christmas" events disappeared in the fifteen years before it was restored and the county was once again ruled by a king: Charles II. This is one of the stranger seasonal stories. Many people do not believe it could have happened when they first hear of the incident, but it did. Christmas had become what the Puritans termed "drunken revelry," and even when they left England and came to America, they refused to celebrate Christmas. Their influence in New England continued until the 1870s when Massachusetts schools finally closed on Christmas Day and students could enjoy the holiday.

ᴼSmallpox Epidemic

It was not religious fervor but sickness and disaster that almost cancelled Christmas in Atlantic Canada some two hundred and fifty years later. The earliest occurrence was in Charlottetown, Prince Edward Island, when on November 13, 1885 the *Daily Examiner* reported that a Doctor Jenkins had seen "several cases of smallpox." Within days dozens more cases were discovered and the province moved quickly to set up an ancient "insane asylum" as a temporary hospital. It was stated in the paper that officials were "not to spare money in their efforts to prevent the spread of the epidemic."

As far as local merchants were concerned, this pandemic could not have come at a worse time of the year; small side-street concerns and huge front-street outlets were stocked to the rafters with Christmas goods. *The Summerside Journal* of October 12 noted that "hotels and stores wear a dreary-deserted look," and on October 20, the *Moncton Times* stated, "business is almost entirely suspended in the affected areas." The *Charlottetown Examiner*, however, said rumours the stores in town were closed had not the "slightest foundation."

Vessels arriving in Charlottetown from Montreal, where it was believed the scourge had originated, were not allowed to unload their Christmas stock, nor were their crews allowed to disembark.

Since it was mid-November, schools had begun practising their holiday music and recitations. These presentations were a highlight of early winter right across the Island, but this year the schools were closed and rehearsals halted. Churches, too, had begun preparations for cantatas and pageants, there being only a half-dozen Sundays until the show would be staged. But these, too, had to cease as churches were likewise closed.

By the last week of November the merchants were beginning to panic and staging sales of goods they *did* have. When they asked the medical board for advice on dealing with the smallpox outbreak, they were told to fumigate their stores daily. Churches began to reopen as Christmas approached, but few were able to stage elaborate pageants or creative cantatas. By December 9 the Summerside paper stated: "The smallpox excitement appears to have subsided. The town is full of country people every day...business generally is good."

With the worst of the disease over by December 10, the medical office provided an update: there had been eighty-eight cases of smallpox and thirty-four people had died, and there were still new cases coming to their attention. However, stores that had been closed reopened, as did churches. Schools, except a few in the countryside that hadn't been exposed to small-pox, remained closed until after Christmas. Thus, Prince Edward Island's first possible cancellation of Christmas was averted.

The Halifax Explosion

When the Halifax Explosion of December 6, 1917, destroyed Nova Scotia's capital, there was not much chance to think of Christmas; the citizens were more concerned with rebuilding their lives and their city. Christmas was, for the most part, the last thing on their minds. Among those hurt in the tragedy were about ten thousand children, some of whom lost their entire families as well as their homes. In the overwhelming magnitude of trauma they could have been easily forgotten, but in a magnificent display of human resourcefulness and kindness, that did not happen. Up until December 21 that year, the children had little hope that Santa would visit Halifax and Dartmouth. However on that day of winter solstice, a bold announcement appeared in the *Halifax Herald* stating, Santa Claus Limited had been "organized to provide Xmas cheer for 10,000 homeless children," and an appeal went out for "money, workers, and automobiles." Six portraits

A patriotic tribute to the end of the First World War. Merchants were certainly happy to see and the return of purchasing.

appeared with the explanation of the endeavour, followed by the words, "You can't refuse THEIR call!" The next day's advertisement noted, "The women of Halifax have rallied nobly to the call to tie up 10,000 packages for the Homeless Children of Halifax," and then added, "but they cannot be delivered unless auto owners—and there are 500 of them in Halifax—donate their cars." The message got through. On December 26, the *Herald* headline proclaimed, "The Kiddies were Remembered in Halifax as Never Before and Santa Claus was Busy All the Time." It was followed by a description: "There were well-filled Christmas trees at Bellevue hospital, the YMCA Hospital, the Ladies' College hospital, and the shelters were not forgotten, for there were also trees at St. Mary's Hall, the K. of C. Hall, Acadian Hotel, Victoria Hotel, Grafton Street Methodist School Room, St. Paul's Hall, the Dwyer home, and other places where those whose homes were destroyed on December 6th are being sheltered." As one commentator noted, "The children will never forget the first Christmas after the great explosion."

Destitute adults were not forgotten either, and likely long remembered the kindness of the travellers from Truro. They had arrived en masse in Halifax and were spotted "unostentatiously slipping crisp bank notes into the hands of some of the older people," according to press reports in the *Chronicle Herald* the day after Christmas.

Their actions, and those of the persons behind Santa Claus Limited and a parallel organization, the Farmer Smith Rainbow Club, ensured there would still be Christmas despite the aftermath of what had been the world's largest man-made explosion before the advent of the nuclear bomb.

The Spanish Flu

The final account of the possible cancellation of Christmas was more widespread. In fact, it could have resulted in the season being scrapped in all four provinces had it not petered out by the end of November. It was what was called the Spanish flu, and it was a worldwide epidemic that had been raging in 1918 and hit Atlantic Canada hardest beginning in mid-October of that year.

There were similarities and differences between the provinces' response to the disease, including how it was tackled, how it was treated, and how medical and government officials dealt with it.

New Brunswick

The first Atlantic mention of the international panic caused by Spanish flu was found in the Saint John–based *Standard* newspaper of September 21, 1918, under bold headline "Spanish Flu has Invaded Canada." The article described "150 Polish soldiers in hospital with the dreaded disease in the Ontario-based Niagara [military training] Camp." It went on to say there had been three deaths, but none among the men in the Canadian sector of the camp.

The following day, a report noted the disease was not causing many deaths in New Brunswick, but that was not the case in adjacent New England. The report went on to list town after town, and city after city, where there were dozens of deaths daily. A Saint John nurse stationed in Boston wrote home to say, "People are dying by the score. Half the nurses in the hospital are off duty sick, and the other half are worked to death."

A companion article stated that there were twenty thousand cases of Spanish flu in the US that week. Moncton was the first New Brunswick city to report cases on September 25, with seven ill. By October 1 in nearby Hillsboro, there were fifty cases reported, schools and churches were ordered to close, and public gatherings forbidden. There were no deaths to that point, but on October 2, Mrs. Albert Christopher, age fifty, became the first victim of the outbreak in Hillsboro.

In Shediac, it was reported that a daughter of Mr. and Mrs. Marcus Henderson, just fourteen years old, had died too.

It was October 5 before the influenza was reported in Saint John, and it broke out among two recruits who had come to the city from Boston the day before. One of them, Jeffrey Fred Rigby, was placed in St. James Street Military Hospital, but died on October 11. He was buried in Fernhill Cemetery, and according to his death certificate his demise was caused by complications from pneumonia and Spanish flu. The day before he died, October 10, the Saint John Board of Health closed schools, churches, and theatres, and declared that no public gatherings were to be held until further notice—which came just over a month later.

By November 13 there were no new cases in Saint John, but some were still being reported from outlying areas. On November 15, theatres reopened after a five-week closure. Two days later, there were nineteen new cases reported in Saint John. Nonetheless, schools were allowed to reopen the following Monday, November 18.

An advertisement for Chapman Bros & Canfield Ltd.

ᴼNova Scotia

In Nova Scotia, the October 16 issue of the *Halifax Herald* carried reports of the Spanish flu in Washington and Toronto, along with local news of the death of two Dartmouth residents. The following day popular social gathering spots like pool rooms, billiard parlours, and bowling alleys were ordered closed as thirty-two new cases sprang up across the city. Two days later, the ban was broadened to impose restricted hours at shops, tearooms, and restaurants. Of the two thousand military men stationed in Halifax, only forty-eight had been stricken with the flu.

By October 21, though, there were five hundred cases confirmed in the city, resulting in three deaths. A building at the corner of Windsor and Almon Streets had been taken over by the provincial health board as a temporary hospital. Outside the city, three deaths were reported in Amherst and a half-dozen in Lunenburg. Yet by October 22 there was mounting public pressure to reopen schools, churches, and places of amusement, as some citizens claimed they were living in a "city of enforced gloom," and that an "influenza epidemic does not exist." This was despite the fact that on October 23, 123 new cases of influenza were reported in Halifax, which the *Herald* stated was a record number, "almost double that of any day since the precautions against the epidemic began." By October 28, the same paper was able to report the epidemic was "seemingly on the wane." On November 4, it was stated "medical men" were in favour opening of schools, churches, and theatres, and on November 6, this happened. Rules stated that most institutions could resume regular hours, but overcrowding on trams was to be avoided, and dance halls were to remain closed. Thus, the worst was behind the city. Normal shop hours meant the public could begin preparations for Christmas.

Prince Edward Island

Though the Spanish flu spread through Prince Edward Island in much the same way as in the neighbouring provinces (that is, via travellers from the Boston area), there were some slight differences in the official response to the sickness.

For example, on Sunday, October 6, 1918, Islanders experienced what the media called "Churchless Sundays," as, due to the threat of flu that had reached the island, public gathering places were to remain closed. No other jurisdiction made as much of these closures as the Island newspapers did for they offered, at no cost, space in their papers for sermons to be printed. The Bishop of Charlottetown, Henry O'Leary, and the Revered Dr. Fullerton took advantage of this in the *Charlottetown Guardian* on October 25, the third churchless Sunday to be observed.

Neither commented on the flu, which by then was thought to be "dying out," yet the same paper noted four deaths had occurred the previous day. In a meeting of the Summerside Board of Health on October 28, the members took a step not mentioned in any of the other Atlantic provinces: "Public funerals shall be prohibited until further notice." In addition, similar to other areas, all stores except drugstores, butcher shops, restaurants, and hotels were to be closed at 6 P.M. on weekdays. On November 1 the ban was lifted, with the exception that the Prince of Wales College should remain closed for additional weeks; public schools could reopen under "such conditions that the school board may adopt."

Further, as acting health officer Dr. Yeo considered there might still be isolated cases of the flu, the Charlottetown Board of Health decided that when there was a known case, the affected residence would be "placarded," this being a warning notice placed in the window. Like the funeral motion, this response was unique to PEI.

Newfoundland

In a Newfoundland and Labrador Provincial Archives online publication "Archival Moment," it is revealed that it was September 30, 1918, when three seamen from a steamer visiting Newfoundland and the "Spanish Lady" (Spanish influenza) first visited that province. The next day, two additional cases were reported. From then on, the epidemic spread across the province. By October 20, the *Evening Telegraph* noted there were forty cases in Fox Harbour, sixty in Long Harbour, and "several deaths had occurred throughout the bay" and the "disease is assuming big proportions."

In that same issue there is an example of how one merchant, Henry Blair, advertised to take advantage of the situation. His promo read, "The Spanish influenza may attack you if, through neglect and getting colds, you allow your vitality to be lowered." Blair's recommendation was Stanfield's wool underwear and keeping the feet dry courtesy of "reliable Canadian rubbers and overshoes." Many merchants like Blair were quick to seize the marketing opportunity as the flu spread; they offered not only clothing and footwear, but a myriad of medicines, such as Scott's Emulsion and Minard's Liniment, or locally produced Dr. Stafford's Gargle. None of the remedies had any demonstrable effect against the malady, which remained a medical mystery to the leading scientific minds of the day.

By October 28, 9 cases a day were being admitted to the Grenfell Hall Hospital. To that date, 138 had been admitted for care in St. John's. Across the province, some 759.

Public closures in Newfoundland were not as widespread as elsewhere. By November 5, schools were closed and public meetings banned, but churches remained open. On Armistice Day, the day peace was declared in Europe, medical practitioners in Newfoundland were being urged to relax quarantine regulations, and they did so the following week.

By November 18, St. John's merchant Bishop, Sons and Co. Ltd. had placed a half-page advertisement of an "Advance Christmas Sales" urging the readers that "New Santa Claus Stock" was ready," and it was "more important than ever before that the Christmas Spirit be kept alive this year and careful selected and useful gifts are the best means to this end."

Indeed, Newfoundlanders had endured a rough fall and more was to come, for through the winter and into 1919, people continued to fall ill. But at least, as the disease waned through November, Christmas 1918 did not have to be cancelled, and those who did not succumb were very open to celebratory events and a visit from Santa.

ACADIAN CHRISTMAS

An English-only writer is at a considerable disadvantage collecting stories of how the Acadians marked Christmas, but through perseverance—and the goodwill of several men and women who shared the stories that follow—it was possible to glean bits and pieces about the similarities and differences that constituted the celebration of the season over the decades.

For the most part, Christmas, as it developed in the latter part of the nineteenth century, was strictly a religious occasion in the Acadian settlements in the Maritimes. At this time, Newfoundland was not a part of the Dominion of Canada, and did not have pockets of Acadians, as was the case in other provinces.

In general terms, the celebration of the New Year was more prominent in this era than Christmas. There was not a lot of commercialism, and if gifts were given at all, they were mostly homemade and attributed to the baby Jesus. A gaily decorated tree was not a part of the observation in most areas, and Santa was an unknown or vaguely mysterious creature.

Some of this will be evident in the accounts that follow, which have been collected either through written accounts or by personal visits to Acadians in New Brunswick. It can only be assumed that their experience paralleled their cousins in the other provinces. The beginning of the story goes way, way back to the early 1600s.

ⓞEchoes from Old Acadia

"Echoes from Old Acadia" was first printed in 1874 in a literary magazine called *The Current*. The actual magazine is not extant, but a copy of the piece was located in file C-27, page 338, at the Saint John Regional Library. No author's byline appears on the piece, but it was not likely written by an Acadian in the opinion of Georges Arsenault, a Prince Edward Island expert on that culture. He suggests after reading the "Echoes" piece it might prove worthwhile to consult his book *Acadian Christmas Traditions* (Acorn Press, 2007), which has one chapter on pre-1870 Christmas traditions and another titled "New Traditions Take Root," which might offer a more accurate picture of early Acadian Christmases. Arsenault pointed out that "Echoes from Old Acadia," which was subtitled "An Acadian Bûche de Noël," must be read as fiction and not a factual early Acadian experience. Nevertheless, it is included, as there are many other bits of fiction in this collection, and every one of them is based on some fact or study that enriches our understanding of Christmases past. Please also

note variations in spelling and accents in this and the other portions of the chapter reflect what was written at the time, not what might currently be in use.

The "Echoes" article begins with a look at the Christmases that the first settlers to Port Royal may have known at home in France:

The Nova Scotia Order of the Good Time.

An Acadian Christmas, in the olden days as now, had many a point of difference from the typical Christmas of France. The Norse blood in their veins gave importance to the Yule log in old Acadian eyes, and the Acadian of this later time, having breathed for generations the electric New World air, has suffered his Christmas to be touched by Anglo Saxon neighbours. On this side of the water it has never been, as in Paris, one of the more carelessly regarded Jours de fête distinguished solely by the scenic splendour of the midnight masses upon its vigil; nor has New Year's Day wholly usurped its role as the day of giving and loving, of forgiving and feasting and being glad.

In what follows, the author seems to have captured what might have happened long ago when the first French settlers were at Port Royal:

Parisian Christmas has always seemed to me a thing consisting somewhat of eau suere and colored tissue paper; but Acadian winters are not propitious to any such light stuff. A glance back two centuries and a half will show us a Christmas which no rejoicing will make mirthful; and in the Acadian cottage of today, we find at Christmas, the hearty and rugged merriment of a people which has reached its simple prosperity through a hard fight and a thousand bitter trials.

It's December 26, 1610, Anno Domini; and the tiny French colony at Port Royal is five years old.

This is the quiet of Christmas morning at Port Royal 264 years ago. No clamouring of bells, no laughing, shrill voices, no idle hurried crowds as in their own dear Picardie and Normandy. Jean de Biencourt, Baron Pourintcourt, has with him twenty-three persons in the little lonely colony. No need of work, or haste this Christmas morning. There is nothing to hasten for, and their work is for a few days done. They have drawn in the Yule log with abundance of cut firewood, and though they have by no means too much venison in store, they have worn themselves out in the hunt and need not take it up again till tomorrow. So they idle about, and Dream of Fatherland, of Child and wife till it shall be time to gather in the chief room of the fort and eat their apology for a Christmas dinner. They are depending almost wholly now upon such fish as they can catch through the ice of the inland lakes, and on the venison they capture for themselves or buy from the friendly Micmacs encamped near at hand. Their grain, corn and barley and a little wheat all but gone; the longed for vessel from France still (delays) delayed; and it is doubtful if they can succeed in staving off absolute famine. But in this one day at least, they will not stint themselves, though venison and fish become cruelly monotonous to their palates.

Last night they had lighted the Yule log with brave cheerfulness and good fellowship, had welcomed in the Feast with firing of guns and had initiated the convert Meniberton with his braves into the blessed mysteries of the season. Father Fresche had summoned them in toward midnight, and mass had been celebrated with single-hearted fervor, indeed, but ah, with what a difference from the services even then, as they knew, being offered up in lighted aisle and chancel far away. They had thought of the sea of upturned faces, rapt and moveless, as the shepherd priests came forward reverently, and the curtain was drawn back to show the Virgin and the Child. Again in their ears rang the scoring, flawless treble of the hidden bay, singing, as an angel, the Gloria in Excelsis. Again, as they chanted with closed eyes, they heard the full responses, the clanging of swung censers; they saw the ranks of surpliced priests and singers bow together; and the aromatic breath of the incense stole into their nostrils. But it was only a handful of exiled and weary men singing at midnight in a rude, half-lighted room; outside their walls the limitless Acadian wilderness, and a thousand miles of wild seas between themselves and home. Then, for some, as they turned to their blankets, what aching hearts to see no little shoe, set out in prim order before the fireplace, expectant of toys and sweetmeats from Jesus Bambin! [bambino?] And for all of them the coming festival could be but a season of longing and looking back. This was their Christmas Eve.

This is followed by a short description of the meal, noting, "The courses are few and little varied." Then it was time for "stories and encounters of wit, and remembrances, and toasts; speeches...with 'A la Clair Fontaine' raised with other loved old songs." As the night fell, "the fire on the wide hearth leapt up redder...ever hissing and sparkling fitfully as they watched the flame intently," until Christmas Day ended and they fell into sleep and silence.

In this same scrapbook is a description of Madawaska County at a much earlier time than that of Audrey Stevenson, and this gives a glimpse of the day-to-day living quarters, the furnishings of same, and the celebratory elements of the festive season. It begins:

In Madawaska County, New Brunswick, leagues inland from the beating of sea winds, on fertile banks of the St. John and Green River, the Madawaska, Quisibis, and other lovely streams, the Acadian now builds snugly his wide-eaved cottage, setting and orchard about it, amid fields of flax and buckwheat, and painting his broad barn doors, and the vane of his inevitable windmill, of the crudest ochreish red. At Christmas, the snow has fallen all around him to a depth of five or six feet, his fences and boundaries are obliterated, his roofs scarcely rise above the white encompassing levels. Indoors, the fire lights up his shelves full of blue and white dishes and glimmers in the wood of walls and doors. There is no chilly plaster to be seen. The ceiling is of wood, darkened with years and smoke; the one partition dividing his abode and sleeping room is of wood, polished like the walls, by the rubbing of hands and shoulders. The massive square bed; the square cradle that rocks with dreadful thud. Loud enough to keep a baby wakeful a whole lifetime; the square lockers; the square table; the square chairs; the square loom; the spinning wheel that could not well be square—all of the same brown, shining wood. And on Christmas Eve, there are guns and shouting, the drive in the pung, half filled with quilts and straw, to mass at the little chapel miles away. And on Christmas Day, the fiddle reigns supreme. Neighbours flock in, and moccassined feet dance indefatigably, morn and noon and night. Huge slices of sweet bread, which has been made for this feast out of plain dough, kneaded up with molasses and spotted with dried huckleberries, are washed down with wholesome beer brewed from spruce boughs and juniper. Sometimes, the national beverage of Canada, rye whiskey, plays a quiet part in the proceedings; but our Acadian does not make a beast of himself. Not seldom, as it grows late, the dancing palls and the singing. Then, as of old, all gather around the fire; and if, as often happens, a modern cooking stove has supplanted the open hearth, they provide themselves with large raw potatoes, from which, with their clasp knives, they shave their slices artistically, and fry them to a turn on the hot black covers; and the sizzling and aroma fills the air. If the hearth still holds sway each arms himself with a slim green sapling whereon he toasts red herring for the damsel of his choice who sits beside him. The children of the home, meanwhile, from under parti-coloured coverlets look through the open door with unwinking eyes, too early exiled from the circle, but solaced with peppermints, and like delicacies, which the good angels, acquainted with the nearest grocery, has brought them in their sleep the night before. So, the day and the night draw to a close, and if the mood of the party has been a merry one the cooks perchance are crowing under the snow-muffled sheds, the last stars fading out in the biting, gray- blue sky of dawn, as the guests race away in a confusion of jangling bells and steam and snorting of the ponies.

The next Acadian recollection is a personal interview and closer to our current era. It was conducted in the late nineties with Clairmont and Jeanne Côté, who were then living in Moncton (though originally Clairmont was from St. Arthur in Restigouche County, and Jeanne from Acadieville in Kent County).

Clairmont's earliest recollection of Christmas would be in his seventh year, about 1940.

We spent the winter in a little camp outside of St. Arthur, about a mile from the Fred Basque Lumber Camp, where my father worked. There was Father, Mother, an older brother, and three sisters. We were all in two rooms. As Christmas approached, Dad would go into town to get some supplies. He'd tell us to go to the bush and get a tree, and we'd make our own decorations. We'd use cardboard to make moons and stars, and cover them with foil from the green tea mom had. We had no lights, but the tree looked good. We hung stockings, and I believed in Santa until I was about seven or eight, but then I started to realize it was our parents.

Due to the distance to St. Arthur, the family did not go out to Midnight Mass on Christmas Eve, but Clairmont recalled, "We went at other times during the winter when a crew would be going into town by sleigh." The family did, however, have prayers on Christmas Eve, but that was not unusual as Clairmont noted: "We had prayers every night: said the beads, gave thanks to God." He did not recall any of the exact prayers from his youth, but at Christmas he remembered singing "Jingle Bells." It was a mix of French and English, he said. "I think it went: Père Noël, Pere Noel, bring us some presents, some candy, and toys." Certainly not the usual words for this old chestnut of the season.

As for the toys, Clairmont said, "There were seldom toys until the later years, after my sister went to work." The stockings were never emptied on Christmas Eve, but on Christmas morning after a long night. "We would get oranges, apples dad had bought, and candies Mom had made, and sometimes socks and mittens she had knit."

, N.-E JEUDI 2 JANVIER 1896

ALLELUIA !

Anges, Archanges, Séraphins, vous tous humains, Césars, souverains, Humbles, grands de la terre, au palais, dans la chaumière, ici-bas, au plus haut du ciel, prosternez-vous, et louez l'Eternel ! Béni soit Jého-vah ! Gloire au Dieu des armées ! Chantez saint, saint, le Seigneur ! que sa puissance et sa grandeur soient aujourd'hui et jour proclamées, et comme il l'ordonna, parlez-ci-eux sublimes dans les abîmes, sur les cimes, Hosanna !

NOEL.

Noël ! Jésus est né !
Étonné,
Il voit, pour lui rend hommage,
Devant son front d'enfant roi,
Pleins d'effroi
Se courber pâtres et mages.

L'étoile qui jusqu'à lui
Leur a lui,
Sur l'humble étable arrêtée,
Mystérieux phare, met
Au sommet
Du toit sa lueur lactée.

Les chérubins familiers
Par milliers
De tous points du ciel accourront,
Divins papillons venus,
Ingénus,
Vers la clarté qu'ils entourent.

Noël ! Comme eux accourez,
Cœurs navrés,
Vers la Foi qui se révèle !
Noël ! Levez tous les yeux
Vers les cieux :
Voici l'Étoile nouvelle !
                          MARC LEGRAND.

NOEL-ETRENNES

L'Évangéline, January 2, 1896.

Even when he was very young, Clairmont would snare rabbits for the Christmas meat pie. "It was traditional Christmas fare," he said, "and was made of pork, rabbit, potatoes, and spices. It wouldn't be Christmas without it," he said emphatically.

Two Christmas games Clairmont recalled playing as a youth were "Borrow" and "Who's Got the Button?" The former was found on the back of checkerboards and was quite complicated, but "Who's Got the Button?" was a simple guessing game and required no special equipment or difficult rules. Outdoor play was all based on cold weather and snow cover; sliding and skiing were his two favourites.

⌐⊙⊙⊙⌐

Two hundred kilometres away in Acadieville, Jeanne's Christmas unfolded a bit differently: "We decorated our tree just as Clairmont did," she recalled, and "hung our stockings and waited for Santa." She added, "I actually thought I saw him once, but I think it was just a shadow." By age seven, an older sister had exploded the myth.

Unlike Clairmont, Jeanne's family always went to Midnight Mass. "We went by horse and sleigh, and we'd be all bundled up in robes, but my, it was still cold at times." While sleighing along, they would sing "Jingle Bells" and some church songs. She recalled one called "Gloria" and another titled "Venite Adoramus."

Following Mass there was an all-night feast, and according to Jeanne, most families in the village would do the same. The main food at the feast in Acadieville was not meat pie but poutine, which Jeanne described as a "mix of raw and cooked potatoes balled around a square of pork or chicken, and then boiled."

One thing Jeannne's family enjoyed that was not found in many Acadian homes of the era was a battery-operated radio, which they listened to at Christmastime and throughout the long winter months.

One memory Clairmont and Jeanne had in common was the elaborate Christmas cards they would receive from relatives who had gone to New England for work. "They were very fancy with lots of glitter," both recalled, adding, "you can't buy anything like them today."

Due to societal changes, you would be hard-pressed to find people with such simple yet meaningful memories of Christmas.

～୦୦୦୦～

However, a few years later, another chance came to do an interview on the topic of Acadian Christmas, this being with retired nun Lauraine Léger, who had grown up in St. Paul, about twenty-five miles north of Moncton. She reflected back to the early 1900s, and said that at that time there were no trees in the homes, nor was Santa spoken of. "That came in the thirties," she said, "when some of the girls who had gone off to the States to work brought those ideas to the village. The first tree I saw was in Cape Bald. A girl came back, and she put up a tree, and everyone—the whole village!— came to see this tree in that house on Christmas Day."

Prior to that, Lauraine said, Christmas was all about the birth of the Christ child.

It was about the Mass. It was the only time we would go out by horse and buggy or sleigh at night. The church was a few miles from home and there were three services on Christmas Eve. We went at midnight. It was really special to be out at night. There would be bells on the sleighs, and you could hear them coming through the darkness. Sometimes the sleighs would be decorated, too. When we arrived at the church, it would be lit up. It was quite a sight. There would usually be a choir, and they would sing carols, sometimes in French and sometimes in Latin.

When the service concluded, people did not rush away "like today, when they scatter for their cars," she said, adding, "the people wanted to see the crèche, and they would be talking to one another and wishing one another a Merry Christmas."

Lauraine's recollection of the evening party following the Mass differed from Clairmont and Jeanne's, as she noted, "Réveillon [Christmas Eve] was not always an all-night affair. There was not always a big feast when I was young. My parents would be tired, and when we got home, there would be some cakes and tea. Later on, it became normal to have a real meal."

In the 1930s, the tradition of hanging stockings began, and Santa began to be spoken of—though, she noted, "Many parents chose to say that the Baby Jesus would bring the child something if they were good." The gifts were simple: "An orange [was] the normal stocking treat, with a few nuts, and candies like barley toys," Lauraine said. When Christmas trees became popular in the thirties and forties, the gifts that appeared under them were also simple: "A school box, a whistle, a pair of hand-knit mittens. When my brother started to work in Moncton, he brought gifts home," she remembered. "It might have been a hairbrush and comb for my doll, still not very big gifts." It was also to Moncton where her Christmas wish list for Santa would have been sent. "My dad drove a bus from St. Paul, St. Marie, and St. Antoine. He told me he'd give Santa my letter when he got to Moncton, so I asked for a teddy bear. I got it. But I suppose dad just threw those letters away, but he must have read it first so he could get the teddy I wanted," she laughed.

As the interview concluded, Lauraine remembered the Christmas tradition of sharing stories, which she said were always part of the holiday gathering in her younger years. "Sometimes it would be an uncle, other times a passing peddler, but they kept the old Acadian tales alive," she said, and proceeded to share her favourite: "Old Dollar,"[1] about a sorcerer who was believed to be an offspring of the Devil. "He could do just about anything," she laughed. "He could put a spell on a person, change into any animal he wished, become a ball of fire, like the will-o'-the-wisp, make people fall off their sleighs. You can imagine how

---

1. Georges Arsenault wrote on this name: "I have published a few legends in my book *Acadians Legends, Folktales and Songs from PEI* about la Vieille Dollar who lived in Prince Edward Island. Her name was Marguerite Dollar daughter of Pierre Dollar. Pierre Dollar had come to teach in PEI and then moved to NB. People referred to him as 'le Vieux Dollar.' He was considered a sorcerer. He was probably born in Europe and according

entranced we were with these stories. The parish priest was not too fond of this, though," she said with a chuckle, adding, "but we'd listen for hours."

Christmas in Madawaska

This account is reflective of more modern times, and is summarized from an article written by Audrey Stevenson when she was a correspondent for the *Telegraph Journal* and *Evening Times Globe* in 1970. It first appeared in the latter paper on December 24, 1970, and as such, gives a glimpse into the Acadian traditions of the season in northwest New Brunswick. She opened her story as follows: "Christmas in the Republic of Madawaska is a happy time; the geographic location gives it a unique flavour all its own. Just across the Saint John River from the state of Maine and bordering on Quebec, the warm and fun-loving people are a blending of several nationalities and cultures, predominantly French."

Continuing, she noted, "During the festive season...Edmundston is a glitter of lights in the shape of bells, stars, snowflakes, candles, wreaths, and trees, mounted on aluminum standards."

Keeping with traditions of the old-time Acadian Christmas, Stevenson noted that at "City Hall and the churches there are flood-lit manger scenes, and choirs of the various churches spend weeks preparing special music as the great majority of people attend Midnight Mass on Christmas Eve." Again, following long-established custom, she describes how the church service is followed by the "Réveillon when family gatherings are held, gifts exchanged, and traditional gourmet foods—especially tourtière [meat pie]—are enjoyed."

Christmas in Moncton

Vera Ayling did a piece for the *Moncton Times* of December 23, 1977, which shows that the customs of early Acadian Christmas were still alive at that time, but they were perhaps not as popular with the younger generation.

to family traditions, was a sea captain. He first lived in Tracadie, Nova Scotia, where he married Sophie Petitpas. He signed his name Petre Daller. His descendants now go by the surname Dallaire."

Her story focused on the Belliveau family of Moncton and it opened with a statement from Mrs. Jeannine Belliveau: "Christmas has always been a special day for the Leopold-Belliveau family...we believe in miracles." The particular miracle Jeannine was referring to that year was her husband's recovery from a severe snowmobile accident. It had taken a long time, but he was hale and healthy at the time of the interview, and was again serving as an alderman-at-large for the City of Moncton.

The couple explained that their seasonal celebrations were "simple and traditionally Canadian," and noted, "for us it is a family day with the children, and we are fortunate that the whole seven of them like to spend Christmas at home with us."

The celebration, they explained, began with attendance at Christmas Eve Mass at Christ the King Church, followed by a drop-in at their in-laws to watch them open their gifts. Jeannine explained, "Sometimes Mrs. Belliveau serves Acadian food; poutine, râpée, or a chicken fricot. It is a treat for us because I don't make them." She further noted that, "I have never made Acadian poutine—boiled potato balls centred with pork; my children don't like them, nor the pastry of meat pies, either," she explained. So, it would seem at least one traditional Acadian custom was not going to survive in the Belliveau home. Mrs. Belliveau did note she made lots of fruitcake, cookies, and squares, which the children did love.

On Christmas morning there was a standing rule that the children were not to wake their parents until eight o'clock, nor could they open their gifts before their parents were up. There was a routine for gift opening, too: the youngest opened their gifts first, and down the line to the oldest opening gifts last.

A customary turkey dinner followed at noon, and then there was relaxation around the lit tree, with some recorded music to enjoy. In the later afternoon, the family would leave home for visits to relatives. "We have a regular family reunion at Christmas," Mr. Belliveau explained.

This concluded the look at a typical Acadian Christmas in 1977, and through what was written, we can look back on half a century later to reflect on what the Acadian Christmas experience was like then as compared to earlier times, and, for Acadians, compare it to how it has changed in the decades that have followed.

L'Évangéline's influence on Acadian Celebrations

Just as the daily and weekly papers of the English press did, the French-language newspaper *L'Évangéline*—first published in Weymouth, Nova Scotia, from 1887 until 1905, and then in Moncton until 1982—had an influence on the Acadian celebration of Christmas. As a weekly, it did not have the advertising revenue or the editorial content of a daily. Nonetheless, *L'Évangéline* always included Christmas-related copy in December, right from its earliest issues. While it is impossible to judge just how extensively it was read, and thus just what influence it did have on celebrations, this can also be said of the English press. Though the English papers capitalized on the commercial aspect of the season to a greater degree than the French press and used illustrations more lavishly, *L'Évangéline* had a more sacred approach to what was fast becoming a secular presentation in English papers. Thus, we see a unique layout in *L'Évangéline* in 1894, with the form of a cross and the words "Anges, Archanges, Séraphins," (angels, archangels, seraphim) inside the cross's boundaries, which clearly indicate the story of the holy birth is to follow. Which is does, issue after issue, in various forms. However, as in the English papers, *L'Évangéline* also included poems about Santa Claus. One that appeared on December 27, 1894, explained that "when Mr. Clock strikes twelve on the cuckoos, in the palace and cottage where people are sleeping, Santa Claus is coming in the white snow." It then noted, "He has toys, dogs, roosters, monkeys, wagons,

L'Évangéline, *December 20, 1916.*

swords, gentle lead soldiers with small hair and dolls for the girls." It goes on to note that "when it is quiet, and the ashes are low...in his long white coat he goes grazing to the fireplace where he fills the stockings from top to bottom." This poem ends with the writer explaining that he lost his own belief in Santa before his fourteenth birthday, lamenting: "This beautiful dream vanished of this amazing man who must be an angel."

Like the English papers of the era, the editorial in *L'Évangéline* issue nearest Christmas Day was always dedicated to the season. Headlines often consisted of a single word, like "Noël." Most years the holiday issue also had a fictional Christmas story of some sort, sometimes a serial, sometimes a stand-alone tale.

The other item in common with papers of the era was *L'Évangéline*'s reports of French school closures for the holiday season. In the first issue of January 1896, it was coverage of the Collège Sainte-Anne, which spoke of the joy of the occasion of the school closing exercises. It then went on to list the recitations given, and the music presented. In between were fourteen presentations in French—and surprisingly, two in English: the first an unnamed selection from Dickens, and the second "The Heathen Chinee" by Bret Harte, a popular American poet at the time.

While it is obvious from the stories of Clairmont, Jeanne, and Lauraine above that not all Acadians had access to the stories and articles of *L'Évangéline,* it certainly had an influence on those who were able to read it, and would have helped to standardize the celebration among Acadians, just as the English press did among other residents of Atlantic Canada.

CHRISTMAS GHOSTS

≈⟨◌◌◌◌◌⟩≈

Other than the annual viewing or reading of Dickens's classic *A Christmas Carol*, ghosts and their stories do not have much connection with the celebration of Christmas today. That was not the case in Victorian times. No Christmas party would have been complete without a ghost storytelling session. They were the highlight of gatherings, and there was a strong belief in their presence and power. If a child was born on Christmas Eve, Victorians believed the child turned into a ghost as they slept on every Christmas Eve throughout their life. If born on Christmas Day, it was believed he or she would be able to see ghosts lurking any time through the year. It was also widely believed that Christmas was the one day of the year that ghosts or spirits would *not* come around—thus, it was a good day to share ghost stories without upsetting them. Dreaming of ghosts was considered a shocking sign that bad luck, loss, or disappointment was imminent. Of course, an audience gathered around a flickering fireplace, winter winds howling about a creaking multi-storey home, helped set the scene. Aged relatives, who had many life experiences, could always be counted on to share an eerie tale as the family gathered to mark Christmas. Today, we do not have the same multi-generational living arrangements, most families don't live in dark Victorian mansions with their candle- or lamp-lit rooms, nor do we do as much visiting with friends and relatives at Christmas. Gradually ghost stories disappeared from Christmas celebrations. In the present age, ghost stories are still popular, but they are more likely to be told around a summer campfire, or at Halloween, when the old standards come forth and are still considered good entertainment, able to send shivers up the spine.

Newspapers and magazines published in the holiday season of yesteryear are a good source for discovering the stories our ancestors enjoyed as Christmas developed in Atlantic Canada. With the lights turned low and a real or artificial fireplace flickering, the ghost stories printed here—the genuine as-written article from the past—can be retold with good effect. Many others are readily available on the internet for those who have an interest in reviving ghost stories as part of celebrating an old-fashioned Christmas.

ᴏPrince Edward Island

The first tale comes from the *Prince Edward Magazine* issue of December 1899. This is a condensed version of the tale "The Phantom Bell Ringers," as told by J. Edward Rendle. It was already a well-known fifty-year-old tale when he retold it, so he subtitled the story "The Ghost of Old St. James," as it occurred in what he described as the "Auld Kirke" [an ancient name for the original St. James church] of Charlottetown, which had been built in 1831:

On an early autumn morning of October 1853, Captain Cross was making his way along the Brighton Road toward the Royal Oak stables where he was to look after a recently arrived horse from his father's estate in Devon. When he reached Black Sam's Bridge, he was surprised to hear what he thought to be a ship's bell ringing. It was clear and distinct to him, and rang eight bells. It did not appear to be coming from the sea, but from the heart of town. As he pondered about just where the sound was coming from, he continued walking, and was soon on Pownal Street where he heard the sound again, and it was at that point he determined it was coming from the tower of nearby St. James Church. This seemed strange to him, as it was too early in the day for the church to be calling its members by ringing its bell, yet he had clearly heard eight tolls. He hurried toward the church to investigate, and as he approached saw three women at the entrance door to the belfry. They were dressed in white material, but had uncovered heads and feet. The women did not seem to take any note of him as he approached. Just then, the bell rang again, and he cast his eyes up toward the louvers in the tower, and in the gap between the slats, he saw the form of what seemed to be a fourth woman. When he looked down to the entranceway, he saw the church doors open and watched as the three women disappeared into the tower and the door closed behind them.

At this point, the church sexton [caretaker], Davy Nicholson, arrived, drawn by the sound of the bells, and he and Captain Cross tried to open the church doors and found them securely locked. Peeking though a small window in the door, they saw the retreating form of the women ascending the steps that led to the bell room.

It took a few minutes until the sexton was able to go to the manse and secure a key to the tower. By then the minister, Dr. Snodgrass, also arrived on the scene. All three men entered the porch, and climbed the stairs to the bell area. It was a shaky experience on a creaky set of steps. The wind blew violently and the tower moaned and shook. The bell continued to ring intermittently. When they reached the bell room, a trap door had to be opened in the floor so they could enter. When they got inside, to their surprise, there was no one in the room. They looked out through the louvers, and saw nothing of any of the women who had been at the tower door. The sexton offered an explanation for the bell ringing, saying it had been the wind, but could not offer any explanation for having seen the women skitter up the stairs, or where they had gone once they reached the bell room. Later, influenced by the minister, the sexton denied having seen the women at all. But Captain Cross had no such pressure put on his story, and maintained he had heard the bells and had seen the women, and it had left a lasting impression on his mind.

Later, it was revealed that many others had heard the ringing at the same hour, though none had seen the women.

A ghostly image of what was known as the Green Lady, November 1957.

So, what was behind the bell rings and the sighting of the four women old St. James? In Rendle's opinion it was more than a coincidence that the bell ringing and the sinking of the *Fairy Queen*, with members of the church on-board, had coincided on that day long ago. He concluded: "In the afternoon of the same day, Friday, October 7, 1853, the sad intelligence was that the mail steamer *Fairy Queen* had gone to the bottom of the sea in the strait between Pictou Island and Cariboo and seven lives lost; four women and three men. Three of those drowned were members of St. James Church congregation." He added that people interested in the strange events of the morning—the appearance of the women and the ringing of the bells—thought it more than just a coincidence. He indicated many people thought Cross had seen the ghosts of the shipwreck victims at the church. "To the above mystery I can offer no satisfactory solution," he finished. "Life—for the present we are but half alive—is full of the marvelous. That we may understand more of the marvelous capacities latent in ourselves, and of the phenomena which surrounds us, is the object for which this narrative has been written."

Rendle's story has lived on. In 2016, Canada Post selected "The Phantom Bell Ringers" as a theme stamp in its "Haunted Canada 3" postage-paid postcard, thus spreading the story from coast to coast.

New Brunswick

Our New Brunswick ghost tale is not a story printed at Christmas, but one that took place at Christmastime. It was shared by Florence Cass in her 1984 book *The Royal Commoners*, and happened on the banks of the Nashwaak River, which flows into the St. John River at Fredericton. The Cass family was looking forward to the celebration of Christmas in 1866. Nuts had been gathered, wood stacked, potatoes and fish stored, rabbits snared and dressed, their furs sold, a caribou caught and butchered, and the mother, Isabella, had made mincemeat for the pies that would be the highlight dessert on the big day. Father Tom was off working at a cash job at a foundry in Carleton, and expected home any day. It was December 20 when Tom appeared. Their son, Foster, was first to see him as he looked out the window.

He shouted to his mother, "Dad's coming, come quick!"

"I will put the tea on," his mother responded.

But when Foster looked outside again, there was no sign of his father. Isabella came to the window, and not seeing her Tom, said, "Where, son?"

Foster replied, "I saw him, Mother. I saw him plain as day." Foster then went out to look for him. There were no tracks in the new-fallen snow. "I saw Father and Bob Evans coming up the road," Foster said. "How can this be?"

He stood on the spot where he had seen his father until his mother came out after him. "You look like you saw a ghost," she said.

"I did, Mother!" he cried out in anguish, fearing the spirit of his father had appeared to him to tell him something—maybe to warn him. They left candles in the windows every night until New Year, but Tom didn't return. No one enjoyed the Christmas season; they only went through the motions. Something was wrong, seriously wrong, with Tom. The thought hung over the family like a heavy cloud.

After Christmas Rick Cass brought a letter from Reverend Huestis, dated December 19, 1866. It read: "Your dear husband has been very sick for the last three days, but you could do no more for him than kind friends are doing. The doctor says his lungs are infected. I felt you should know of his affliction."

When the letter was read, Foster said, "I knew it; I saw him."

He looked at the date—the nineteenth.

"I saw him the day after Reverend Huestis wrote this letter, Mother."

Isabella replied, "Dad went to our heavenly home for Christmas, but he came here first."

Later, the family received a clipping from a Saint John newspaper that confirmed Tom's death on December 20—exactly the day his young son had seen him walk up the lane to their house.

Nova Scotia

The *Halifax Herald* and its Christmas Supplement of 1887 contained not one, but three macabre stories. One was about a ghost in Halifax; the second was set among the tombs of a graveyard at Annapolis Royal; the third featured ghosts and witches around Parrsboro.

The first was titled "A Thrilling Ghost Story," and was centred around Citadel Hill. The second, "The City of the Dead," was subtitled "Echoes from the Historical Tombs in Canada's Oldest Graveyard." The third story, "Ghosts and Witches," had no subtitle.

While the first and last are readily identifiable as in the ghost genre, the second alludes to belonging in that category, but does not deliver. Instead, it is an interesting read about a French burying ground of Nova Scotia's first settlers, and what the author has learned about those buried there from reading the names and epitaphs.

The other two are summarized here. They can be read online in full, or at libraries and archives that have issues of the now-defunct *Halifax Herald* on microfilm. There are surely many other ghost stories that would show up.

So, to the first of the stories and to the famed Halifax Citadel, where the storyteller is identified as Uncle John, he tells his young audience of a severely cold night seventy years earlier when his grandfather was on watch duty. He was responsible for visiting the different guards stationed about the town, one of which was at Queen's Wharf downtown. "Halifax," Uncle John pointed out, "was perhaps the gayest town of its size in all the British possessions." Now, on the night in question, Uncle John's grandfather had been reading a book during the evening and the time had slipped away. When he closed the book, he heard the Duke of Kent's clock strike twelve, and realized he had not made his rounds. He hastened to get around to the various stations without further delay. Just then he heard a

Telling ghost stories.

heavy tread outside his room. He got up, looked around, but found nothing and no one…not a soul was stirring, and all was quiet. He closed the door and turned back into the room. As he did, he sensed the door was reopening, and indeed it was. In glided the figure of a man dressed in the uniform of the heavy dragoons. The figure stared at him, and caused his hair to stand on end, his teeth to chatter, and though he wanted to speak, he found he could not. The figure glided across the room and when it got to the bedroom door, it pointed with its gloved hand in the direction of the town and spoke one word: "Come!" At that point, the figure disappeared out the window, leaving in its wake a bright streak like a current of electricity. Uncle John's grandfather then buckled on his sword, threw his military cloak over his shoulders, and proceeded to make his rounds. He crossed the drawbridge over the moat, instructed the sergeant to turn in the guard, and was striding at a great pace toward the northern glacis of the Citadel, when he noticed the figure there, keeping pace with him. The grandfather was a remarkably temperate man even in those days of deep drinking, so knew he was not under the influence of anything. But he also knew what he was seeing was not a human figure. He began to feel his knees shaking and giving way under him but nonetheless, screwed up his courage and said to the figure, "Rather a cold night, my friend."

The figure turned toward him, scowled, and in a rumbling tone replied, "I don't mind the cold. I like it. I like moonlight nights, too, it's cheap." Then the figure warned the grandfather, "Don't touch me. If you touch me I won't answer for the consequences. Many a man has been found dead in the morning from being so rash, and no one knew what was the matter with him, and a jury would come to the conclusion, 'Died by visitation of God.'"

At that revelation, the grandfather took out his sword and shouted for help with all his might. A corporal soon came running, his sword drawn and ready for battle. Then such a din arose such as was never heard before. The figure's eyes fairly flashed like an electric arc of light, his sword gleamed like King Arthur's renowned Excalibur, and a battle lasting a full ten minutes ensued. Soon, another rescuer came to the grandfather's aid, but it was not as the reader might imagine. As the grandfather made one final thrust at the ghost, he suddenly found himself on the floor of his own "comfortable quarters." Once on the floor, he realized he had dreamed the whole thing. Still, he expected to hear the shouting of the hobgoblin he had fought; instead he heard the fifes and drums sounding the reveille, ushering in the glorious festival of Christmas. Later, on reflection, his ghostly hallucination was attributed to the stuffing in the turkey.

⁓ↈↈↈↈ⁓

Writer S. D. Scott wrote "Ghosts and Witches" especially for the *Herald*. The introduction indicated the story is one of the "romantic traditions of old-time tragedies along the Parrsboro shore." Scott began his discourse by claiming the person who had originally suggested the story to the *Herald*'s editor would have been more qualified to share the story, but undertook the task anyway. He opened the tale by saying, "The Cumberland ghosts are of two classes: one of which we may call 'Real Estate Ghosts,' and the other 'Portable Ghosts.'" He explained the first were so designate because they stayed near the site of their tragedy, and "show[ed] themselves to suitable travellers." The second are the "personal property of the murderers or other parties connected with the crime." He pointed out that "several haunted men have lived and died in Parrsboro, and their ghosts have departed with them."

Then he went on to identify some ghosts of the area, the first being the "Fork Woods Ghosts." This ghost, he explained, was known to sit upon a rock in the forest—which stretched unbroken for a mile in each direction from his perch—and terrorize those who passed by. The rock itself had been destroyed when Mapleton was colonized, but there were "two or three disembodied inhabitants of their earthly homes" still seen in the area. There were ghosts to be feared in the "Boar's Back, and the Haunted Mill" at Parrsboro, and on the road to Advocate Harbour. In this area, too, Scott noted, "There are many spots to which the sprits of the departed were of late wont to return." As an example, he included the story of a "precipice by the highway down which a carriage rolled with its human freight, [which] had its well known ghost." Then there was the shipyard where a "woman's form appeared almost every evening throughout the summer, moving lightly and mysteriously about the framework and staging, and passing securely over perilous places." This was not a quiet ghost, for, as Scott noted, she "sang songs—wild songs—which were heard by scores of neighbours and passersby."

His article continued with the tale of a man murdered by the pirate Captain Kidd on Isle Haut, and finished up with the story of a Parrsboro family "skilled in witchcraft," and of "the human associate of the Prince of Darkness."

Not much in the way of the macabre was missing in his account. And to think he did not believe he was the best one to tell the tale!

Newfoundland

Parson's Xmas Annual for the year 1899 is the source of our Newfoundland tale. According to information from the Centre for Newfoundland Studies, there were seventy-four Christmas annuals produced in the province between 1882 and 1930. These included *Christmas Bells, Yuletide Bells, Christmas Record, Christmas Review, Colonist's Xmas, Holly Leaves,* and the one in which this story was found, which was printed on three occasions from 1899 to 1901. Though there may be many more ghost stories to be found in these annuals, there are no known copies of many of them to consult. An ongoing search is being conducted to correct this deficiency, so keep checking the Heritage Newfoundland website, as any day there may be something new—or should we say something old—to read.

⋖◌◌◌◌⋗

ⵔThe Camp Ghost (True, so Jim Says) by E. M. White

'Twas on the bank of the Salmonier River, we had a good day's fishing; not a rod in the lot did duty for less than ten salmon, and now we lay us down to rest to enjoy the weed and the cup that cheers, and belch forth our fishy exploits of the day. Each of us failed to take the biggest fish in out of the wet; but as we are of the earth, earthy, let it pass; each one has his fault, singular in his lot who exceeds not the singular number. Plural is the rule, singular the exception; but Jim was a rare exception, while others talked he did business, and looking beamingly at us over a glass of "special" produced again the moss-grown bottle, and bailed like a boat, the ten-year-old nectar, radiant in its blushes to find itself so guzzingly appreciated. And as the fluid flowed, one of our number mused, and musing grew poetical over the scenic grandeur of our encampment (I believe there is in human nature generally more of a fool than of the wise), and watching the shadows and portrayed in the stream, fanned by the bland zephyrs, and primed by the Scotch, the veil of enchantment over him rises, when he attitudinizes and delivers himself of the following: "Boys," Bacon hath said, "whosoever delighteth in solitude is either a wild beast or a god."

But Bacon never had the pleasure of being in the Solmonier woods, or he would have held that the various associations of this green valley are essentially impressive on the human. The winding streams, the noisy waterfalls, the melody of the forest songsters, all joyous in vibrant chorus, the leaves, the trees, their banners of green unfurled, and twilight insensibly fading, all, all, I say unconsciously instill in our thoughts the realization of that beautiful ideal—the religion of nature.

A ghost makes a visit, November 1957.

On arrival we found the fires all aglow, thanks be to good old Jim. There was a magic charm about the home, and a luxurious warmth and comfort about the place. Supper being over, song and story was next in order, and as Mulrany said, "They thawed progressively." And in the thawing they told more of their lives and adventures than I am likely to find room for here, but, in the height of the hilarity; Whizz! Luzz! Every one stood to attention, as this uncanny sound disturbed the air outside the "tilt." Jim passed his hand abstractedly through his iron-grey hair, his face looked worn of the sound again, he raised himself with a jerk, looking a pitiable object with his cap fallen over his eye. He smiled ogreishly in our faces, getting never a smile in return, but only a pitiless stare, but the sun of his sociality soon recovers from the brief eclipse, and shines again.

As he wiped his mouth with the back of his hand, he said, "Gentlemen, that was the voice of a real dead ghost, this tilt is his home." And, pointing to the bank on which I lay, "And that, gentleman, is his resting place."

All hands were for the story—the ghost! the ghost!—when Jim said, "In your patience possess ye your souls," and then launched into the story from the moment Mr. Ghost first entered the tilt, up to the time he left its doors.

Three years ago a professional gentleman from the city was up at the falls with me, and when we were ready to turn in, says he to me: "If I die before you, Jim, I will come back to this tilt some night and see you." I never thought of it until one night I was here by myself, when by the livin' farmer, what should I hear but the lad coming along, and when he stopped he laid his rod against the end of the tilt. I could hear the water rattling in his boots—swish, swish—every step, and the next thing he flopped down a darned big load by the door, and by the holy fly, it shook the tilt. Then, by the good day, I rushed to the door, and pointed my long bazoo [gun] full into his face, and I says: "If you are for good come in, but if not, go off in the divil's holy name." Then he said, "Pray for me, Jim. Pray for me!" In he walks, sans dremonie, and suddenly a man before me stood. Not rustic as before but seemlier clad, as one in city court or palace bred.

"The old man had found you out, Jim," says he, as a curious set expression swept across his face. He was close shaved, and his mouth was set as if his upper lip had been for years familiar with a great moustache. There was a twinge at my heart and I caught my breath with a gasp, only for a moment, and then I was myself again.

He appeared excited and restless and it seemed quite impossible for him to settle down to any purpose when—presto!—down he flops before the fire, and seesawed himself to and fro, watching intently as each separate dying ember, wrought its ghost upon the floor.

Then suddenly he said, "Never again be here alone, as this is to be my nightly abode for years, and the hours of my weary vigil are from night's inception until night's candles are burnt out and jocund day stands tip-toe on the misty mountain tops. Though a rash promise made you when in the flesh, this is my purgatory, my hell upon earth, and I make this vow now, solemnly and determinedly, to wit: If I come upon you here again, by the power vested in me, I shall bind fetters upon you that will chain you to my spirit-body. Out of kindness he was so nice—through the length and breadth of my pilgrimage."

With that he gave a horrid scream and suddenly sprang into the bed beside me, and when next I remember breathing, my wife was gently fanning me, not here, but in my own good bed at home.

There, gentlemen, is my story, and so you, Mr. William Tuck, you are not superstitious, for the joke of the thing you would come here again, and alone; very well sir, you contend there is a superstition in avoiding superstition, when men think they do best by going farthest from the superstition, but, catch me in this tilt alone, never."

⇐⊙⊙⊙⊙⇒

So, now the challenge is before you to share these or other such tales, so that Dickens's A Christmas Carol is not the only ghost story told at Christmas this year or next. And should you wish to share a different Dickens ghost tale, look up *The Story of the Goblins Who Stole a Sexton*, and see how much of *A Christmas Carol* you can recognize in the story of Gabriel Grub, written in 1836–1837, just a few years before the more famous tale featuring Scrooge in 1843. Some say Grub could have been a relative of Scrooge... see what you think!

CHRISTMAS SNIPPETS

There have been many happenings at Christmas that did not become customs, but were unusual promotions, social activities or ways of marking the season that simply have not fit into any of the sections of this book. This chapter will be devoted to pointing out some of these, such as free railway passage for shoppers, employee's presenting lavish gifts to their employers, and a strange request made of children by Santa. They were, at least once, a part of the season's celebration and they could be again, should someone wish to follow up on the ideas.

A Free Railway Trip to Shop

It would be rare today for a shopping centre or merchant in the centre to provide free passage to potential shoppers, but it did happen at least once on Prince Edward Island. On December 21, 1890, a sketch of a PEI smoking steam engine drawing several passenger coaches appeared in the *Charlottetown Guardian*. Under the drawing was an invitation, which read: "All aboard for Paton's & Co. Great Christmas Bazaar." This was followed by the unusual offer of free passage on the railway from Tignish, Summerside, Georgetown, Souris, and all points on the line to the Charlottetown store, where then it pointed out, "Everybody given a chance to see our Xmas Decorations and Mammoth Stock of Dry Goods."

Dance the Night Away

The *St. John's Evening Telegraph* of December 24, 1883, had an item that demonstrated the people of that era had more stamina than we do today. In a piece about a community dance, it read: "It is the custom of many of our people to celebrate the Christmas holidays with music and the dance." It continued by describing an event at the "Star of the Sea Hall," where it stated, "Decorations and refreshments are all of a character to please," and that "an uncommonly fine band will furnish the music," and there would be "an enjoyable time until daylight does appear."

A Curious Custom Best Forgotten

"A rather amusing scene was witnessed at Kelligrew Station by the passengers on Tuesday morning's outgoing accommodation train," began a column in the *St. John's Daily News* of December 28, 1899.

It went on to explain that a resident of the community was spotted on the beach in the process of mending his boat on St. Stephen's Day, which is now generally known as Boxing Day. As it was the rule that anyone caught working that day had to "pay for the offence by treating everybody in the neighbourhood to whatever drinks were called for," the men of the community were witnessed taking action to ensure the custom was carried out. They loaded the offending person into a "fish barrow that was lying nearby," and "proceeded in the direction of the nearest public house where drinks were called for."

As the same custom was in place for "Old Twelfth Day"—as in, the twelfth day of Christmas: January 6—there is a pretty good chance that no boat repairs were done that day by anyone in Kelligrew.

Christmas Wedding

This December 25 wedding took place in Sackville, New Brunswick, yet was found in the columns of the *Summerside Journal* of January 1, 1885. Perhaps it was unusual enough to have made intra-provincial news; Christmas weddings were not uncommon in the early days of settlement, for only an Anglican priest could legalize them, but those days were long past. Perhaps there was a PEI connection at the New Brunswick ceremony, though that is not made clear. Nonetheless it fits this section of different Christmas activities, as it read, in part, "On Christmas morning an interesting event took place in the Black Memorial Chapel of Mount Allison College, Sackville, NB—the marriage of the daughter of the President, Dr. Inch, to Professor Hunton. [...] After the service the happy pair, with their many invited guests, adjourned to Mount Allison College, where they sat down to a sumptuous luncheon. The presents are many and valuable. The couple left on the afternoon train for Boston."

Snail Mail on PEI

Long before the term "snail mail" was coined—indeed, as far back as 1889—there were complaints that mail on Prince Edward Island was moving too slowly. The *Charlottetown Daily Patriot* carried the complaint in its December 20 issue, as one unnamed correspondent wrote, "The carelessness of our Post Office is becoming unbearable...a letter posted in Charlottetown on the 12th, addressed to Malpeque [thirty-six miles distance] reached there on the 19th, only a week in transit. The state of affairs cannot long continue."

Relief of Widows and Orphans

On the night of December 23, 1893, the *Charlottetown Patriot* had a notice that showed the benevolent spirit that prevailed that Christmas due to a tragedy at sea. The notice read: "Remember the meeting in the Stipendiary's Courtroom tonight, to take steps to relieve the widows and children of those who perished in the wreck of the schooner *Grace Parker* at St. Pierre. Let us all who hope to enjoy a happy Christmas give liberally of their means to this humane work."

Now *This* Would be an Invasion of Privacy

All hotels in the Atlantic area freely provided the names of those staying in their establishments during the later part of the nineteenth century, and in some cases, well into the twentieth. Such lists were not considered confidential at that time, though if one did not want his or her name bandied about, they could, and did, provide *nom de plume*. However, this list is typical of what was done and was published in the *Charlottetown Guardian* of December 26, 1911. It clearly shows who stayed at one of the city's leading hotels of the time, which was the Queen Hotel. And that some of them had travelled some distance to reach the capital of the province. The list included W. T. Anderson and G. Wightman of Montague; Mr. and Mrs. Gillis of Nova Scotia; and a M. G. Gosberg, of Saint John, New Brunswick. It also noted those who had stayed the day before, which included guests from quite some distance, with three from Montreal and one from Alberta.

Christmas Shoppers Surprised by 1872 Incident in Halifax

Christmas shoppers on the downtown streets of Halifax saw a scene that will not be repeated in modern times but was not uncommon in the era before the motor vehicle. It occurred on December 20, 1872, according to a report in the *Daily Reporter* the next publishing day. It read: "Chipman Bros horse ran away on Lower Water Street this afternoon and dashed through Hollis Street South and barely escaped colliding with a horse and sleigh standing in front of the Scotia Bank. The horse was stopped at that point by a bystander."

Things I Must Have Dreamed

The *Halifax Evening Reporter* of December 26, 1874, listed a number of items that were true of Christmas then, and, to a large degree, still are to this day. It included:

- That "not a drop of liquor could be obtained in the city yesterday."
- That the "City fathers celebrated Christmas Day by giving the poor people of Halifax a banquet at Temperance Hall."

- That the "congregations in all the city churches were very large yesterday morning."
- That there were "no mammas awakened before daylight yesterday morning to look at Christmas presents, which had been left by old Santa Claus during the night."
- That the storekeepers gave their assistants a holiday from Thursday night till Monday morning.

ꙮAge at Which Belief in Santa Ends

"St. Nicholas, who went about on Christmas Eve and filled stockings by descent through innumerable chimneys, was formerly believed in by boys and girls until they were twelve or fifteen years of age. Now it is a dull child of eight who has not exploded the whole story in the most cold-blooded manner." This is as reported in the *Halifax Morning Chronicle* of December 25, 1888. Surprisingly, recent studies across North America have found that the strongest age of belief is under six, and that the average child stops believing at eight years old.

Children's annual Happy Hearts.

ꙮEmployers Remembered by Their Employees

The above headline comes from the *Sydney Post* of December 26, 1901. Such headlines were typical of post-Christmas presentations to managers, which was common at the time. Although this may still take place today, it would never make into the columns of current newspapers. As it was, the accompanying article read: "The office staff and the Traffic Department of the Dominion Coal Co., Glace Bay, presented Mr. Wm Coyne, Traffic Manager, with a very handsome silver water pitcher, on Christmas Eve. A brief address was read by Track Master Graham, signed by all the members of the Department. Mr. Coyne was taken by surprise and responded to the address, thanking his staff for their thoughtfulness and assuring them of his appreciation."

Santa's Strange Request of PEI Children

The *Prince Edward Island Magazine*, published from April 1899 to January 1905 by Archibald Irwin, included some sixty-seven issues. Among them were six Christmas Numbers. However, one of this publication's strangest holiday stories was not in a Christmas issue at all, but the October 1901 copy. In that month, the magazine had a picture of Santa and a letter in which he noted he "hoped to get to the Island in December," and that he had "a full line of the latest novelties and toys." Santa had a special request for children of the Island: he wanted them to ask the provincial government to remove a twenty-dollar tax they had placed on visitors to the Island. That, of course, included Santa. He warned the kiddies it meant he would have to "slip in during the nighttime to try to get clear" of the new tax, so that he could fill the "biggest stocking you ever can get on Christmas Eve."

The editor of the this St. John's Christmas Number stated it was the first in Atlantic Canada, but as will be discovered in this chapter, the claim was not correct, with Halifax being first.

It could have all been an elaborate play on words, though, since that is exactly how Santa operates. Additionally, no record of such a tax could be found in the legislative reports of 1901.

1919 School Closing Recital

At a meeting of the New Brunswick Historical Society on December 10, 2005, participants were asked to share Christmas reflections from their past. Mabel Fitz-Randolph was one of the participants. She was then in her early nineties, and recalled a one-room schoolhouse closing for the holiday break at South Musquash, where she recited the following poem:

> *Santa Claus, Santa Claus,*
> *Jolly little man.*
> *Down the chimney comes tonight*
> *Fast as ere he can.*
> *Christmas Eve, Christmas Eve*
> *Will soon be here.*
> *We are very happy now*
> *'Cause Santa Claus is near.*

She also recalled her brother Elmer's poem, which went as follows:

> *The camel has nine stomachs,*
> *I heard it at a zoo.*
> *I'd be contented if I had two:*
> *One for Christmas pudding*
> *And one for ice cream, too!*

A Royal Surprise at Christmas

The popular "Man on the Street" column of the Saint John *Evening Times Globe* prided itself on reporting offbeat items discovered in the area. This one surely fits, and appeared on December 27, 1937. It described in great detail a pre-Christmas meal at the venerable Royal Hotel at King and Germain Streets, which wasn't that unusual. What was unusual was the statement that followed: if Saint Johners happened to "drop into the Royal Hotel Friday morn, they got a free meal." It went on to explain that it had been the hotel's custom to serve a luncheon "on the house" for one day during the Christmas season and explained, "there is no advanced announcement to the public for obvious reasons that the management does not want the establishment mobbed. Don't get all excited," the columnist warned, as "it won't happen again for another year."

Christmas Tree on Wheels in Moncton

Atlantic Canadians are famous for their hospitable nature, but few would go so far as travelers on a train out of Moncton at Christmas in 1883. The following reports appeared in the *Moncton Times*, December 27, 1883: "Some of the passengers on the afternoon express from Halifax yesterday decorated a tree in the second-class car with empty bottles (supplied by the commercial travelers and others), oranges, apples, jack-knives, and other articles too numerous to mention. The tree looked first-class and as may be imagined, was a center of attraction. A married couple were onboard on their bridal tour and the tree was in their honour."

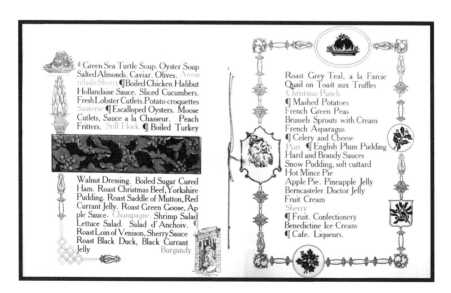

Royal Hotel menu.

A Biblical Christmas Advertising Curiosity

A St. Stephen merchant had a curious advertisement in the December 2, 1866, issue of the *St. Croix Courier*. It began, "The 21st verse of the 7th Chapter of Ezra has all the letters of the alphabet in it, and the 19th chapter of the second book of Kings and the 37th chapter of Isaiah are alike, but you can find a greater variety of choice in family groceries at Jas. A. Bixby's St. Stephen than the Israilitish Kings or Isaiah or Ezra ever dreamed of." No doubt his customers pointed out to him that first verse referred to is missing the letter *J*.

Hints for Christmas 1888

From the Charlottetown *Daily Examiner* of December 18, 1888, some gift-giving advice that might not be understood or welcomed today:

"A champagne cork enrobed in a red flannel ball dress and gilded makes a handsome pen-wiper for your literary friend."

"Do not forget to send your rich aunt a prize Christmas card."

"A receipted dressmaker's bill is a nice present for a wife to give her husband."

"The best thing for the forty-year-old maiden is to give her dilatory lover a hint."

Under the Holly Bough

The poems that were written in the Victorian era were meant to be read aloud at social gatherings, and often they were heart-tugging sentiments. None is more poignant than Charles Mackay's "Under the Holly Bough." While it appeared in newspapers almost annually after it was written in England in 1851, this particular version comes from the December 1903 issue of *Prince Edward Island Magazine* in a piece called "Christmas Thoughts" by George J. MacCormac. He began, "The loving sentiment imprisoned in the holly bough and transmittable into every language can hardly be more happily expressed than in Charles Mackay's verses:

Ye who have scored each other,
Or injured friend or brother
In this fast-fading year;
Ye who by word or deed
Have made a kind heart bleed,
Come gather here!

Let sinned against and sinning
Forget their strife's beginning,
And join in friendship now;
Be links no longer broken,
Be sweet forgiveness spoken,
Under the holly bough.

Christmas Donut Instructions

The *Summerside Journal* of December 19, 1894, ran an advertisement from a Montreal firm, N. K. Fairbanks, aimed at all those who were planning to make the favourite Christmas treat of the era: donuts. They suggested bakers would be surprised at the "delightful and healthful results," if they used "Cottolene, a new vegetable shortening," when making their Christmas donuts.

They provided only rudimentary instructions alongside the words, "To Make a Doughnut" inside the hole of the donut; they knew well that every young cook would have received training from a mother or grandmother, as the donut had been a Christmas treat from the time of the first settlers to the area.

What followed does not make sense to a non-cook, as it said: "Take a hole and put some dough around it, then fry in lard." This was followed by a warning: "This simple recipe has brought thousands to grief, just because of the frying in lard, which, as we all know, hinders digestion." The article concluded, "In all recipes where you have lard, try Cottolene; [...] the young, the delicate, and the dyspeptic can all enjoy the regular family bill of fare."

The Maritime Farmer produced in Sussex, New Brunswick, from 1895 to 1979 often gave details on old-time customs and recipes, and a commentator at Christmas 1971 added to the details above, backing up the popularity of donuts as a seasonal treat. It was a reflection on a turn-of-the-century Christmas, in which the author, Gwen Turnbull, noted: "Every preparation was made for a befitting celebration. The girls and their mothers were unremitting in their work in furnishing a bountiful supply of pies of all kinds, cakes, and donuts. In that day, the donut was the king of the feast: fat, juicy and crisp, and well cooked and wholesome. Some old fellows carried donuts in their pockets and ate them at all sorts of unseasonable hours, and I hear of some families who made them by the barrel."

ᴐDressing a Christmas Tree in 1892

Though not all homes at this date had adopted the custom of erecting an evergreen in the home, for those that did, it's not as if there were Dollar Stores on every corner where decorations could be readily procured. Thus, any decorating advice was welcome, and this short description in the *Yarmouth Light* from December 22, 1892, gives a realistic behind-the-scenes look at what was done. "A Christmas tree ought to be selected with special reference to the space it is to occupy; one with the branches firm, not too broad, not quite tall is best." (People to this day make the mistake of procuring a tree much too large for their living rooms.) The piece continued: "The upper branches should be decorated before the tree is set up, in case they are too tall to be reached by stepladders." (This might have worked before the days of electric lights, but would be difficult to execute these days.)

Then came the decorating. When you see a Victorian-era Christmas tree all decked out, it is easy to see why the method described here became the norm. The procedure began by "tying upon the tips of the boughs white cotton-batting snowballs, short loops of popped popcorn, stings of cranberries," and then mentioned "glittering ornaments, etc." So there must have been an opportunity to buy some glass globes in local stores, that likely copied the success of the F. W. Woolworth Company, which became famous for these in the early 1880s. A calming piece of advice followed, as the write-up made sure to note, "The decoration of the tree many be more or less elaborate as desired."

The final instruction is not something done now, but was the popular way Santa distributed gifts back then, and that was to tie gifts onto the branches of the tree for Santa to pull off and pass out. The advice ran: "To save expenses, yet at the same time to insure a brilliant effect, it is a good plan to hang the gifts so that the bright, contrasting colours may set off the tree. Bundles done up in brown paper are never pretty; but dolls, bright-covered books, gaily painted toys, bright silk handkerchiefs and white scarves, sleds, wagons, etc., should be placed in prominent view."

The final step for decorating a Christmas tree in 1892 was to "sprinkle frost powder upon the tree branches," and then wait for Santa Claus to come and be the "dispenser of candy bags and bonbons." The advice concluded, "If he [Santa] has a fund of Christmas stories and songs to mingle with the gifts, he is all the more welcomed."

Free Matinee for Children of Charlottetown

Movies were the newest novelty in the first decade of the twentieth century, and in Charlottetown, children were introduced to this new amusement for free on Christmas afternoon of 1908. It was a wonderful opportunity at the New Wonderland Theatre. The film reels had been held up due to icy conditions in Northumberland Strait, but the theatre's management was able to screen three features: *Forsaken*, *Never Again*, and *Over the Hill to the Poor House*. They were on the screen between four and five o'clock. *Forsaken* was described as the story of a young girl leaving her poor mother and running off with her lover.

Her disconsolate mother tries to end her life by throwing herself off the balcony of her home. Passengers in a passing automobile come to her rescue. Among them is her daughter and man she ran off with. She takes her mother back to their home, and things are patched up, and the movie ends with a wedding of the couple, who receive the blessing of the mother as a bonus. *Never Again* is about a man's misadventures while on a trip to Coney Island. Well-known sights were often used in the early movies, as people could relate to them wherever they lived. The final movie of the day, *Over the Hill to the Poor House*, is not described in the editorial copy of the paper, but is pretty well self explanatory, and was likely another heart-tugging it-could-happen-to-you feature that made up most of the earliest attempts at movie making.

Boys Beware!

Snowball fights have long been popular amusement among children, as can be discerned from short filler in the *Fredericton Reporter* of December 31, 1879, which described a Christmas-week incident in Saint John that could have had a tragic outcome: "The habit among boys of snow-balling is assuming too great proportions to be allowed to continue. It seems like second nature to some boys to throw snowballs at people when driving, and it is a wonder serious results do not follow. An enraged omnibus driver in St. John is accused of discharging a revolver into a crowd of boys one day last week, the ball entering the hip of one of the lads, and this should prove a warning to the boys who every day annoy citizens on our streets and frighten their horses."

A Word for the Children

Advocacy for children is not something new, as can be seen from a report in the *Fredericton Reporter* of December 24, 1879, when the editors took the school board to task for keeping the students in class almost to Christmas Day. They wrote: "We would suggest to the Board of Education the alternation of the regulations so that the schools should hereafter be closed a few days before Christmas. The minds of the children are naturally upon everything else but their studies, and in many instances they are allowed to remain at home, in which case their standing in their classes is interfered with, while if they attend, their minds are more or less distracted from their studies. The little things look forward to this festive season with feelings of anticipation and delight, and it seems hard to deprive them of all the pleasure it affords."

Sabbath Christmas in Sussex

David Henderson is an indefatigable collector of Kings County happenings, and always does a column in the King's County Record related to Christmas. His 2008 column hearkened back to Christmas 1937, and gave several glimpses at the look of the community at that time. He noted in 1937 it had been a green Christmas, but "despite the absence of the traditional mantle of snow, there was, if anything, a more lavish display of Christmas decorations this year than there was last year. Verandas in many parts of town were bright with Christmas lights. Stately candles burned in the windows, very few homes failed to display the festive Christmas wreath in the windows, and there was hardly a home but showed the spirit of the festive season by some form of decoration."

One observance David noted would seem strange to us in this more secular age and that was how the community marked the twenty-fifth. Christmas having fallen on a Sunday, in many homes those gathered around the trees only opened presents on December 25, saving their "turkey dinner and plum pudding until Monday." Thus, they observed the time-honoured commandment to take a day of rest on the Sabbath.

New Brunswick's "White Christmas" Connection

Many people love the song "White Christmas," and know that it was sung by Bing Crosby in 1942 and was a last-minute Irving Berlin addition to the movie *Holiday Inn*. What many do not know is that Crosby's roots can be traced back to New Brunswick. That information is found in a 1998 article written by Harold W. J. Adams for Cadogan Publishing, which stated Crosby's maternal grandparents, Dennis Harrigan Sr. and Catherine Driscoll, came to the Miramichi from Ireland in July 1831. Crosby may never have known a White Christmas in Hollywood, but his ancestors sure did; the Miramichi is one of New Brunswick's snowiest areas.

Santa Turned Back at the Border

In mid-December 1946, a disappointed Santa—AKA thirty-two-year-old Ben Buffett—was on his way by foot from St. Stephen to his hometown of New Waterford, Nova Scotia, after being refused entry to the United States at the border. It had been his hope to be the first Santa to walk a thousand miles from his home to his American destination. As he travelled, he donned the Santa suit in each town and village to entertain, and hopefully get a place to sleep for the night.

First Christmas Television Shows

It was December 1954 when the first television shows celebrating the Christmas season were seen by Atlantic Canadians. They were programmed by CHSJ—based in Saint John, New Brunswick, the area's first television station—which had began its programming on March 24 of that year. Some features first shown that Christmas are still shown to this day, such as *The Littlest Angel* and *A Christmas Carol*. Other shows and performers are but a memory, such as the Leslie Bell Singers and Jackie Gleason, but good memories for those who saw the first shows and are still living to tell about it.

Charles Dickens in Saint John!

Was this headline on a column in the *Morning Telegraph* of December 24, 1867, designed to lead readers to believe the famed writer was in town? He wasn't, though he wasn't far off; his ship had passed Nova Scotia on its way to Boston, and Dickens had been invited by telegraph to read in both cities.

The headline played on the public's knowledge of his whereabouts, although it was not Dickens who read in the Mechanic's Institute but senator-to-be John Boyd of Queen Square, whose reading "completely carried away" the audience. It was a reading Boyd did many more times, not only in Saint John but also through the province and into Nova Scotia.

Boss Gibson's Generosity

On Christmas morning of 1883, every resident of Marysville, New Brunswick, had a turkey delivered to their door from mill owner Alexander (Boss) Gibson, and every chorister who showed up at the Marysville Church received a gift of twenty-five dollars. Two years later, Gibson greeted one thousand residents at the door of his new mill, as they entered to enjoy a Christmas banquet, which newspaper reports of the era noted "exceeded anything before attempted."

SOMETHING UNIQUE at CHRISTMAS in EACH PROVINCE

⟨⟨⟨⟨⟨⟩⟩⟩⟩

Though plenty of what has been (and is) done to mark Christmas is universal, there are local variations that have been adapted from time to time, and place to place. In compiling this record of how it all began and how it progressed, there was at least one item that stood out from each province that seemed unique, and thus the idea for this chapter was developed. These are at least four items that fit this category, but no doubt there are more.

New Brunswick: The Christmas Mountains

William Hamilton's book *Place Names of Atlantic Canada* has but four names with a connection to Christmas. Of those, only one has a definitive link with an interesting story that can be shared. It was told by your author in the December 1981 issue of *Canadian Living* magazine in a feature titled "Canada's Most Christmassy People":

> *Don't be surprised if you hear children from New Brunswick telling their friends that Santa lives in their province. They have come to their information honestly, because for sixteen years, Arthur Wightman of Fredericton has been telling them the old bearded gentleman has a place all to himself deep in the New Brunswick woods.*
>
> *Santa's Maritime home is known as the Christmas Mountains, and it was Wightman who gave the 2,000-foot peaks grouped around North Pole Mountain their names: Mount St. Nicholas, and Mounts Dasher, Dancer, Prancer, Vixen, Comet, Cupid, Donner, and Blitzen.*
>
> *Wightman says the names were thought up just before Christmas in 1964 when he was employed by the provincial government as a cartographer. "We were trying to come up with the names for a group of nine mountains which were in a horseshoe shape around a previously named peak called North Pole Mountain. As the strains of the song, 'Rudolph the Red Nosed Reindeer' drifted through the drafting office, it occurred to me that Rudolph and the names of Santa's other reindeer would be very fitting for the hills."*
>
> *Ottawa, though, didn't agree with the name Rudolph, saying it was too commercial. "They don't have a sense of humour up there," Wightman claims. "They take everything so seriously. So, instead of Rudolph, the ninth mountain became Mount St. Nicholas.*
>
> *"I'd like to see the Christmas Mountains set aside as a wildlife sanctuary. A place where people could find peace and goodwill away from this chaotic world. That," says Wightman, "would complement my names and could really be in keeping with the spirit of the season."*

Since Mr. Wightman was interviewed in the early 1980s, the area has been subject to some clear-cutting, which would be a disappointment to his dream of it becoming a wildlife sanctuary. Further information can be gleaned from author William B. Hamilton's data on the topic, which located the mountains as being north of the Miramichi River in Northumberland County. He also states that the appellation "Christmas Mountains" as a general term for the cluster of hills (which are part of the Appalachian range), was popularized by writer David Folster, who was adept at promoting the province's historical and natural attractions.

Newfoundland:
The Christmas Cake Lotteries

Perusing the advertising columns in papers of yesteryear can reveal a lot about the type of goods that were available for gift giving. There was a wide range of items promoted: from petticoats to pianos, books to banjos, coal to china cups. Among foodstuffs, the most common adverts were for coffee and tea, fresh eggs, sweet oranges, turkey, geese, and hams. The social events promoted included theatricals, visits to St. Patrick's Crib, and many musical offerings by church and secular singers.

One different item that was found in the Newfoundland papers was the promotion of community cake raffles and cake lotteries. The earliest one spotted was a typical 1.5 x 2 inch insertion in the St. John's *Evening Telegram* of December 22, 1882. It read: "By permission of their worships the Stipendiary Magistrates, R. J. Callanan will hold his Christmas Cake Raffle on Friday and Saturday nights. Raffle to commence at 7 o'clock."

A year later, an unnamed writer was looking back on how Christmas had been celebrated fifteen years earlier, and mentioned "a Christmas card was [then] utterly unknown." Christmas merchandise had also been comparatively rare, as were Christmas cakes. "Now, what tons of toys," he noted, and "currants and raisins and festive things in general [...] more Christmas goods today than the whole island contained fifteen years ago."

So, we can assume from this information that the custom of cake raffles or lotteries began sometime in the early 1880s.

The December 20, 1883, issue of St. John's *Evening Telegram* had three firms promoting their cake events, namely: Hillary's, Bowring, and Kenny's, the latter having rented out the Mechanic's Institute for a Saturday evening event. The phenomenon began as early as 1860, and was a way for the many bakeries in St. John's to market their sweet goods. Before the Great Fire of July 1892, it is believed there were over ninety bakers in St. John's. The cake lotteries were so much a part of pre-Christmas celebrations that the season was nicknamed "cake lottery season." It was so ingrained that the 1864 Act of Suppressing Lotteries was amended to allow the "large and elegantly decorated stock of Christmas cakes" to be sold by chance.

By 1885, some customers began to find fault with the auction process. Under the anonymous name of "Fair Play" one potential cake buyer wrote to the *Telegram* on December 17. His argument was that there was "collusion between a party in charge of the cakes and a confederate, by which the winner was cheated out of his right [to the cake]." This was done, he explained, because the dice were swept off the table before the customer could calculate the total, and the cake would be awarded to whomever the lottery person wished, rather than to the rightful winner. "Most people consider the matter too trifling to be made the subject of inquiry," he noted, further pointing out it was "difficult to corner the cheat." He concluded his letter by saying he was "obliged to you, Mr. Editor, for giving me space to ask for remedy for this matter."

As nothing further was reported in the press, whether Fair Play's letter had any result is unknown. What is known from the advertisements and the editorial supports is that the lotteries continued to be popular. In 1888, the *Telegram* carried this review:

The cake lotteries and the Christmas Numbers of the newspapers are taking possession of the field and challenging the attention of the public for its investments. The dividing line which separates the advent days of Christmas from the holidays themselves seem to be obliterated when the cheery newsboys shout their annual announcements and the bakers, grocers, butchers, greet the eye with their respective displays. As to the lotteries, there are three on the tapis, one, that of Callanan's cakes for tonight, and two, Mr. Wilson and Mr. P. J. Patterson's for to-morrow night. The first named comes off at the corner of Duckworth and Cochrane streets, the second at the Mr. M. Bastow's sale room, Beck's Cove, and the third at the Total Abstinence Hall.

After the great fire of 1892, which destroyed many bakeries, the unique Newfoundland idea of cake lotteries gradually died out.

Prince Edward Island: The Boston Boxes

In his book *An Island Christmas Reader*, author David Weale's story, "A Christmas Box," shares the details of an almost-forgotten element of Christmas for many Islanders: the receipt of a box of goodies at Christmas from relatives working in the eastern United States.

In an article in *The Island Magazine* of spring-summer 1977, author Alan A. Brookes refers to a 1904 article from the same magazine, which estimated some 31,000 Islanders (out of a population of 108,000) had emigrated to various points in the United States, with about 50 percent of those settling in Massachusetts. On the Island, these relatives were often said to be living in the "Boston States," and when they sent packages back home, they were referred to as "Boston Boxes."

Most who emigrated expected to return to the Island, but as they became more established in their careers, as Brookes put it, "It was no longer economically feasible to return." However, they could and did help those back home by sending money or packages.

As Weale points out, the "Boston Boxes" augmented the practical gifts those on the Island often received, like "a pair of mittens or socks knit by grandmother, a rough hand sleigh made by father, a doll's dress sewn by mother out of familiar cast-off materials or a pair of skates with straps made from old harness fashioned by the local blacksmith. But they didn't expect anything fancy or extraordinary. Even the fudge was made right there in the kitchen stove and the ice cream on the back porch."

To compose his story for *An Island Christmas Reader*, Weale interviewed Islanders then in their eighties who shared memories of receiving the boxes. One lady was alarmed when a box she picked up "began to emit strange noises." This turned out to be a doll that could cry, but she had never heard of such a thing. Another man recalled receiving boxes of clothes and thinking, "American boys must have awfully long legs," because the pants he received "always fit in the waist, [but] the legs were too long."

After hearing stories right up to 1990, when one lady Weale interviewed received what she considered the last "Boston Box" (her relative by then too old to send them), Weale composed the story that follows, which, as he says at the end, is based on a true tale. It is called "Silver Lining."

It was just a week before Christmas, 1948, on a small farm in Mount Hope, near St. Peters. It had been a lean year, and there was no money for presents for the seven children; however, a box, filled with second-hand garments, few of which actually fit any of the youngsters, had arrived at the farm from relatives in Boston, as it did every year. The mother of the children decided the best she could do for presents that Christmas was to get out her scissors, and needle and thread, and attempt to 'make-over' some of the clothes so they would actually fit her children.

Every night after the kids went to bed she pulled up close to the lamp at the kitchen table and began the process of tearing apart and sewing back together, weeping occasionally for the want of anything better to give them for Christmas.

On the third night of her work she pulled out of the Boston gift-box a man's well-worn leather jacket with a cloth lining. It looked like something she could make over for eleven-year-old Lou, who was big for his age.

Soon after she discovered, to her surprise, something sewn into the lining. It was a heavy-duty envelope of some kind, and she imagined instantly there might be money in it. Then smiled at her silliness.

There was no name on the envelope and she wondered for a moment whether she should open it, but her curiosity got the better of her. With her scissors she sliced it open, and was almost unable to believe her eyes when she saw that it was indeed money, or what looked like money. But the bills were unusual—the fives, tens, and twenties all looked the same—and she wasn't certain they were real.

She called her husband up from the cellar where he was grating potatoes, and his jaw dropped when he saw the American currency, realizing instantly it was genuine, and by far the largest amount of money that had ever crossed the doorsill into their house. The amount, he said, was sufficient to buy presents for all the children, with enough left over to pay off the mortgage, and perhaps buy a small tractor or car.

Alas, he was spending it before she had even decided they could keep it. She was as principled as she was poor, and was unable to overlook the inconvenient fact that the money was not theirs. She could not imagine spending it without first trying to locate the owner.

Over her husband's protests she went immediately to the home of neighbours and called the aunt in Massachusetts who had sent the box. The clothes, she was informed, had come from a used clothing store and there would be no possible way of discovering who had owned the jacket.

"Merry Christmas, Irene," said her aunt. "That money is yours. And by the way, how much was there?"

"I don't know," replied Irene, "I haven't counted it yet. I'll write you after Christmas."

And she did write, and included in the letter $100 – a token of gratitude for what she had discovered in the lining of that jacket. And for the rest of her life she often wondered – with a poignant curiosity tinged with uncertainty – what stranger had put exactly $1,000 in that brown envelope, and why. And would he be happy or sad that it had found its way to her.

[Inspired by a true story and reproduced with permission of David Weale, Charlottetown, PEI.]

Nova Scotia: The Boston Common Tree

Across Nova Scotia throughout the year, there is a constant consciousness of the province's most unique Christmas custom: the forty-to-fifty-foot evergreen tree sent annually to Boston, Massachusetts. It was first given in 1918 as thanks to the city of Boston for the outstanding aid its citizens provided in the aftermath of the Halifax Explosion a year earlier on December 6, 1917. Though there was no follow-up tree after 1918, the custom was revived in 1971, and the 2018 tree will be the forty-seventh consecutive memorial gift from Nova Scotia to Boston.

When the tree is lit in late November, it's a grand ceremony involving the mayor of Boston and the premier of Nova Scotia. It is Boston's official tree-lighting ceremony that signals the beginning of the Christmas season in the city, with trees throughout the Boston Common and around the city also lit at that time. The ceremony is broadcast by television station WCVB, and receives wide coverage from the print media; in fact the city's two leading papers, the *Herald* and the *Globe*, are actually sponsors of the event.

That night is the culmination of a year-long search for a suitable tree. Thus, for some people in Nova Scotia, the Christmas season is never far from their thoughts. These are the people who keep their eyes open for just the right tree. It has to be fir or spruce, between forty and fifty feet tall, healthy and in good colour, medium to heavy in density, uniform and symmetrical, and accessible. If anyone has or knows of such a tree, they report this to

The Christmas tree lighting ceremony at the Boston Common, 1978.

the Department of Natural Resources, who make the final decision. With great ceremony, the tree leaves Halifax on a flatbed truck, and winds its way through New Brunswick, Maine, and New Hampshire before arriving in Boston. Once in the Massachusetts city, the Boston Recreation and Parks Department raises it in the Boston Common, and adorns its branches with about seven thousand twinkling lights.

The 2017 lighting was particularly significant, as it marked the one hundredth anniversary of the Halifax Explosion. "We will never forget the kindness bestowed by Bostonians," were the words of Nova Scotia's Minister of Natural Resources Margaret Miller when the tree was cut on Cape Breton Island. It's a Christmas season sentiment that will continue to be applicable for decades to come.

GLEANINGS FROM HERE and THERE (And a FEW of MY OWN EXPERIENCES)

There is so much left that could be said about the ways the Christmas season has been marked, but all books have a point at which they must conclude. To do this in this instance, some items have been selected that either amplify what has already been covered by taking a different viewpoint or present a new facet of Christmas. Finally, there are a few short stories that will clearly show the author's own experiences over the past six decades or so.

Labrador Children Who Know No Santa Claus

Dr. Wilfred Grenfell began visiting Labrador by ship from England in 1893, and subsequently established a permanent year-round medical missionary hospital at St. Anthony in 1901. It is widely stated that he introduced the celebration of Christmas to the most remote areas. This article he authored in the *Family Herald* of May 24, 1911, gives some information on Christmas, and illustrates the condition of Labradoreans when Grenfell first came to the area. Besides medical aid, his mission's aim was to improve living conditions through education and agricultural and industrial development so residents could become more self-reliant.

In 1981, the work of the mission was turned over to a government agency (the Labrador Grenfell Regional Health Authority), but the International Grenfell Association is still active in the area, and provides grants to nonprofit agencies that improve health, education, and social welfare.

Grenfell's 1911 article began:

"Doctor, we ne'er seen so wunnerful a Christmas afore!"

This was the common remark that greeted the doctor last winter as he went about the various houses and small settlements along the Labrador coast in the guise of Santa Claus. A small spruce tree dragged over the snow by komatik and dogs, and decorated as best we could in some tiny kitchen, called forth much happiness and gratitude, not only from the children, but from parents as well. It is hard to imagine the land where the children, though of English and Scotch extraction, never have heard of Santa Claus or Father Christmas or never have seen a doll or a penny toy. The trained kindergarten teacher who came to help us last summer said they had not the faintest idea how to skip the rope or play games and hardly knew their left hand from the right.

All along the Labrador coast they are cut off by ice and snow from all communication with the outside world from November until June. Their only chance of hearing of civilization is by an occasional and perfunctory dog mail, which does not carry papers and parcels. Even in summer there are certain places which the mail boat only visits once or twice. Moreover, the houses are placed at long distances apart, often purposely, that the furring ground of one man may not encroach on the territory of his neighbour, who, for this reason, may be sixty miles away. There are practically no schools to serve as social centers, except in the larger settlements, where the predominant religious denominations – Methodist or Church of England – may supply one. These schools are open only for short periods so as to eke out the services of the ill-paid teacher by distributing him over more space.

The people in Labrador are peripatetic in the sense that they move to one locality for the winter and another for the summer, according as either place is nearer their means of livelihood. Thus, the winter house, or shack, is close to the furring ground while the summer residence is on the coastline so as to be within easy reach of the fishery. The average winter house contains only one room, which has to serve as kitchen, dining room, smoking room, and not infrequently bedroom for the entire family. In fact it is not an unusual thing to find two families sharing one house. Visitors are always welcome, even though they may be obliged to sleep on the floor. As a general thing, the family sleeps in little wooden berths, like cupboards, which are built in the wall. They regard heat as their friend and cold as their enemy, with the result that almost always the windows are nailed in and the door kept religiously shut. Under such circumstances, what can be expected of the children?

I have been told by grown men that they never in their lives had a complete bath. A change of underclothing is an exceeding rare occurrence. I remember one patient, when I first came over from England, who I wished to have taken a bath before admitting him to the hospital. I had taken over a tub from home and left the room after telling the man what to do. A few minutes later, I returned to find him getting in with his boots on. He explained that he always had supposed that their purpose was to keep water out.

The food of the average settler is very simple. Breakfast consists of "loaf" and tea, and, if the family is prosperous, of molasses and butter also. The latter, however, is much too great a luxury for the children, for they have to make a few pounds of the cheapest oleomargarine do for the entire winter. One of the nurses at St. Anthony's hospital this year asked a little girl if she had a nice Christmas.

"Oh, yes," replied this child, "I had an apple all to myself."

It is hard to conceive how the natives exist on the diet they have. No wonder a great amount of tuberculosis exists from semi-starvation. Imagine trying to bring up children without a drop of milk obtainable with the nearest cow several hundred miles away, and canned milk – which is selling at a almost prohibitive price of twenty-five cents a tin—at the store perhaps one hundred miles away, and then they may not have it always.

As soon as the boys are old enough (and old enough means about twelve years of age) they are sent to help at the winter's work, such as driving dogs and komatiks 'round to the traps and hauling firewood. The children "grow up" very early in Labrador, in fact, they have almost no childhood. After the day's work is over, the family may be too poor to buy a lamp, and I myself have examined patients by the light of a sputtering, smoking piece of tow laid on a lump of seal fat.

Every day is like every other, except as the winter wears on, the family, instead of having tea and molasses, is obliged to subsist on dry flour alone. In the spring, the settler moves out to his summerhouse to get ready for the fishing season. For once the fish have "struck in," the whole atmosphere is changed. Then the work of the year begins. Often as early as two o'clock in the morning until dark, the men are hard at work catching, splitting, and cleaning the fish. Even the tiniest children, as well as the women, help in the latter occupation.

We are trying to make a special effort in Labrador to have the children in even the smaller settlement supplied with teachers so that they may be instructed in the rudiments of reading, writing, and arithmetic, and also that the teachers themselves may be versed in the fundamental principles of hygiene and sanitation.

At St. Anthony, in northern Newfoundland, where we have our largest station, we have established an orphanage to accommodate forty children. There they are given a thorough education, especially along mechanical lines.

New Brunswick: Joy to the World and the Reed Family

Most readers of this work likely have some connection with the sea. No one in Atlantic Canada lives very far from the ocean that washes the shores of our provinces. Thus, this tale of one man's experience with the sea at Christmas might bring the image of some offshore fisherman to mind.

Christmas, it is said, is ever old, yet ever new. The same may be said of stories. This fictional story is old—yet may be new to you. It comes from the pen of Chester A. Dixon, a storyteller from Deer Island. It was written for a Christmas issue of the *Fundy Fisherman*—one of many periodicals Dixon submitted his stories to in the 1930s through 50s.

Dixon was born on Indian Island, one of the 365 islands said to be in Passamoquoddy Bay and lived his early years there, but when all permanent inhabitants left the island, he moved across a channel to Cummings Cove on Deer Island. His many pithy articles were based on his intimate knowledge of the life of Passamaquoddy Bay fishermen and he knew whereof he wrote, for he worked with them and lived among them. Whether this story is based on an actual event or just Dixon's fertile imagination is hard to tell. When you have read it, you will think that surely there must have been some incident that precipitated the tale. Perhaps it will even remind you of the famous Dickens story that is so popular during the Christmas season. In condensed form, this is Dixon's story:

Henry Reed and his wife, Marion, lived on a tiny island off the coast of Charlotte County that had been inherited by Henry from his father, who had lived alone with his only child after the death of his wife. Henry had been to the mainland only once while he grew up. He had never known the joys of Christmas, because his father had become bitter about all things Christian since the loss of his wife, and had taught his boy to hate the very name of Christmas Day.

At twenty-one Henry found employment on the mainland at one of the fish canneries. There he met a girl, Marion Bliss, who later became his wife. Soon thereafter, his father died and Henry decided to move to the island with his wife

One year, a week before Christmas Day, Henry went out fishing as others in the community went about preparing for Christmas. Henry became so engrossed in his fishing that he failed to notice a big black cloud that had appeared in the northwestern sky. The long undulating swell of the ocean seemed to have taken on a greasy aspect.

"We're going to have a squall," Henry thought.

Little did he think it would turn out to be a raging blizzard. Darkness fell. The storm grew worse—so bad in fact that Henry, for the first time in his life, became uneasy. His thoughts turned to his wife and children back on that isolated island.

"What if anything should happen to me?" he thought. "What would become of them?"

For the first time in his life Henry gave serious and studied thought to things religious. Though he had never prayed in his life, spontaneously, simply, words of supplication to God fell from his lips. He asked for God's mercy upon him, and upon his wife and children. Hardly had the prayer been uttered when a giant wave lifted the boat skyward and tossed the craft aside until it was almost on its beam-ends. Henry felt sure the boat would capsize, but it righted and he managed to grasp the tiller and get the craft straightened out before the wind.

"That was a close shave," Henry thought.

Just then a strange thing happened. Henry was certain he heard someone saying to him, "What about Christmas now, what about Christmas?"

The phrase seemed to be burning itself into his brain.

The hail became fiercer than ever. The little boat and its occupant seemed to be doomed. The waves rose higher and higher. The wind howled. But the sound of the persistent question still rang out in Henry's mind: "What about Christmas?"

"I'll promise you, God," Henry cried out, "that I'll celebrate the first Christmas in my life with my dear ones, if you'll save me!"

Scarcely had his covenant with God been made, then a distinct lull in the wind took place, although the sea seemed as angry as ever. Henry's boat was half-full of water. He increased his pumping efforts and although his little craft was wallowing dangerously in the trough of the sea, no more waves came aboard. Before long, the wind abated considerably and after a few hours had passed. It changed and blew from the south.

Henry Reed unfurled his sail and headed for home. Although it was past midnight when he arrived, his wife was up and greeted him with great joy.

The following day Henry Reed went to the mainland. He had plenty of money with him and he bought Christmas toys, trinkets, candy, and fruit for the children and lovely presents for his wife. He also purchased trimming for a Christmas tree, and fitted himself out with a new suit of clothes.

That was the Reed family's first Christmas, and not Henry's last as he thought it might be while on his boat in the bay just days earlier.

Nova Scotia: Christmas in our School

The third story originated in Cape Breton, Nova Scotia, and was written by F. A. C. of Sydney for the December 16, 1908, issue of the *Family Herald and Weekly Star*. Anyone who has memories of attending a one-room schoolhouse will relate to this author's experiences, which appeared in the "Teacher's Column" of this widely read publication.

Those who did not attend a one-room schoolhouse will also find this a nice comparative piece to their own Christmas experiences, for whether the school was big or small Christmas was a highlight of the school year. It began:

Now, I am not exactly what you would call a "bright" teacher and I fear my description of our last year's Christmas celebration will not be very original, for it was only my third Christmas in the profession, but if it may interest some other young teacher I shall be very glad.

My grades are III and IV, and from the first of December I was besieged with questions from my forty pupils: "Please, Miss, will we have a Christmas tree?" and "Please, Miss, will Santa Claus come?" I only said, "Wait and see."

Each morning I began with a little half-hour talk relating in some way to Christmas: one morning it was about sheep and shepherds; another about camels and so too the Wise Men; another about Santa Claus in his imaginary workshop; then Christmas in other lands. I found the children never tired of talking about little Italian children and their good "Befana," or of the French, who received their presents in a shoe. And lastly, the story of the little Christ child, and why we celebrate His birthday.

I found the time well spent while learning eight or ten songs—even yet, the children ask to sing "Little Bethlehem," or "Away in a Manger."

We had our Christmas tree on Thursday afternoon, the nineteenth, and at the beginning of that week, I asked the boys to bring evergreens [boughs], with which to decorate the schoolroom. They got a fine large tree and we had it set up two days ahead so it would be nice and dry by the time we needed to use it.

Everybody was anxious to help in some way, and while the girls strung popcorn at recess time or before school, the boys helped me cut spruce and tack it up.

We made several wreaths of "mon's paw," twined with artificial holly around barrel hoops. These were for the windows. We hung them halfway down and they looked very pretty both from outside and in.

I tacked branches of spruce all around the room-doors and windows, and twined twisted strips of red crêpe paper about two-and-a-half inches wide with it. All this, you see, is very inexpensive. I bought one of those long fancy-coloured festoons, which occupied the place of honour in front, draped over the picture of the King and Queen. Then we had a half-dozen large red bells in different places.

But to come to the tree. It looked just like every other Christmas tree, but oh! the children thought it was the very nicest one they ever saw. We dismissed at eleven o'clock and I had from then to two to decorate, so no one saw it till the bell rung for afternoon school.

Three days before each child cut a little a little stocking-shaped booklet out of fancy paper and we wrote invitations to the fathers and mothers. The outside was decorated according to the owner's ability with a spray of holly, and I can tell you, some of those stockings were very elaborate indeed. I had drawn a number of Christmas sketches on the blackboards and the program of songs, recitations, and dialogues was done in fancy lettering with coloured chalks.

You may depend everyone was present to the minute, and everyone remembered his piece. By and by, just as we happened to be singing "Santa Claus is Coming," a loud jingling of sleigh bells was heard in the hall. How the eyes brightened! For no one knew what was coming. Nearer and nearer it sounded and then the door opened and in came Santa. Everybody knew him at once, for he looked just like his picture. He walked up and down the aisles, patting one, then another on the head; and he certainly acted his part splendidly. Then as I handed him the gifts, he called the names; as each child came forward, he handed him the gift with some funny remark.

All too soon for some of them, he said he was afraid Dasher and Dancer and the other reindeer would run away if he did not go to look after them, so amid jingling bells, he left with a promise to come back next year.

One of the school commissioners and one of two other gentlemen who were present said a few words, and then with a closing song, our celebration was over. As the children passed out, I shook hands with each one, and wished him or her a happy vacation.

Did I enjoy this afternoon too? As much as any of those forty eager folks in Cape Breton, Nova Scotia.

Prince Edward Island:
The Christmas Orange

And now to Prince Edward Island and author David Weale's story of the humble orange, which may be the most oft-recalled memory of old-time Christmas in Atlantic Canada. It is from his collection *An Island Christmas Reader.*

In collecting the stories for this volume, one of the most common stories was in regard to the delight of receiving an orange in the toe of a Christmas stocking. This seems to have been common in all four provinces, among rich or poor, country or city folk, English or Acadian. David Weale's sharing of this facet of Christmas seemed to say it all:

Perhaps the greatest difference between Christmas today and Christmas years ago is that back then people were poor. Not that there aren't any poor today, but then everyone was poor—or almost everyone. It wasn't a grinding, end-of-the-rope kind of poverty. Most everyone had food enough to eat and warm clothes to wear. The woodshed was filled with wood, the cellar with potatoes and carrots, and the pickle barrel with herring or pork. There were strings of dried apples hanging from the attic rafters, and a carcass of frozen beef hanging in the shed. In many ways it was an era of plenty, so you might say that rural Islanders weren't "poor," they just didn't have much money.

What strikes me forcibly when I speak to some older people is that the scarcity of money made it possible to receive very great pleasure from simple, inexpensive things. I know, for example, that for many people, an orange—a simple orange!—was a Christmas miracle. It was the perfect golden ball of legend and fairy tale which appeared, as if by magic, on December 25th. In that drab homespun world of grey and brown, it shone mightily like a small sun. According to one ancient legend, an anonymous benefactor dropped gold coins down the chimney of a poor family and they accidently fell into a stocking that was hanging near the hearth. The chimney orange of later centuries was said to represent the gold in the toe of that stocking.

The orange was a kind of incarnation of Christmas itself, and for many Islanders, the most vivid evocative memory of the blessed season is the memory of an orange on Christmas morning. One woman from a large family in Morell said that at her home you were fortunate if you received a whole orange for yourself. She recalled some lean years when she received half an orange, and was happy for it.

For children who ate oatmeal porridge for breakfast virtually every day of their lives, and had molasses on bread most days in their school lunch; for children who looked at fried potatoes almost every evening for supper and considered turnip scrapings a special evening snack; for those children, an orange was a marvel, something almost too wonderful and prized to be eaten—an exotic sensuous wonder.

One woman confessed that she kept her orange for a week after Christmas, kept it in a drawer. Several times a day she would go to her hiding place and take out the orange just to fondle it and smell it, and to anticipate joyously the pleasure that was to come. Eventually it had to be eaten: deliberately, unhurriedly, ceremoniously, and gratefully. Piece by piece, and finally the peeling—it was all eaten, and it was all good. All that remained was the hope that there would be another Christmas and, if God would be so kind, another orange.

On the opposite side of Nova Scotia from the school story on Cape Breton Island, we go to Yarmouth for our story number five.

Nova Scotia: The Spirit of Christmas

An unidentified writer for *The Yarmouth Light* of December 21, 1905, gave a general overview of Christmas at the end of the nineteenth century in that western Nova Scotia community. What is recalled is important as a source that verifies what has been shared in other sections of this book. It shows that Christmas experiences were much the same no matter where they occurred throughout the Atlantic region as Christmas developed into what it has become today. Some highlights from the article follow.

At family parties, time passed slowly. "The family parties were held at Christmas and New Year, the former at Grandma's and the latter at Aunt M's were something we youngsters looked forward to from one long year to another; the years were twice as long then as now."

On Christmas morning, a long walk: "We were awake of course, before daylight, and by nine o'clock, we were washed and dressed in our best clothes and ready with a dozen other cousins for a three-mile walk to Grandma's. There were often twenty of thirty aunts, uncles and cousins."

At dinner: the children watched while the adults ate. "The children were everywhere but at the table and were often consoled by a slice of rye bread, with thick cream on it, or a donut till the older ones were done eating. [...] We hung around the kitchen [and] we witnessed the surrender of turkey with dismay and looked hopelessly on as goose after goose disappeared, leaving only the carcasses, necks, and drumsticks with an occasional pope's nose. [...] It was often nearly four o'clock when we children filed into the dining room [...] for our dessert, which by that time was reduced to a solitary raisin here and there left in a saucer."

After dinner, it was ghost tales. "As it began to grow dark, but too early for tea, we would steal across the fields to Aunt D's and persuade her to tell us ghost stories. We would feel creepy all over and be afraid almost to retrace our steps in the gloaming lest we meet a walking ancestor or see somebody's double."

Santa seemed so real "We were not worried over Christmas gifts weeks before the day. We left all that to Santa Claus who we knew, never forgot us, and the smallest trifle from him was gratefully received. [...] How real everything was to us then: Santa Claus was no myth. He was the spirit of Christmas then, and he is the spirit of Christmas today. We may call him friendship, love, remembrance, or what you will, but he is now, and ever will be, the Spirit of Christmas."

Christmas as I Remember it on Inner Wood Island

This island is located in the Bay of Fundy about two miles offshore of Grand Manan, New Brunswick, south of the village of Seal Cove. It is about two miles in length and a half-mile wide. No one lives on the island today, but there were several families eking out a living when these memories were made almost a century ago. The author is Audrey Ingalls, who was well into her nineties when these memories were recalled.

Christmas planning began with the arrival of the Eaton's catalogue...there was so much wishing. Our parents would be having hushed conversations, and would make hurried trips to Eastport, Maine, by boat of course. The mail boat would arrive on our island and bring so many big bags of mail, but none for us.

As the month of December passed we would be preparing for a Christmas concert at the school. It was not allowed at the church. The concert was so exciting; a magical and mysterious and beautiful occasion, it was a child's dream world.

At our house, I remember the cozy warmth of the coal burning in the Quebec heater in our living room. The isinglass in the iron doors allowed light and shadows to flicker around the room, birthing great imaginations. Our tree was so carefully chosen, and shone with pretty ornaments, wax candles, tinsel icicles, and garlands. Realistic snow was made by whipping Lux Pure Soap Flakes into a meringue-like consistency, then slathering it over the tree branches. Later, as spills dropped, we made villages under the tree with tiny ornaments, houses, people, and animals.

On Christmas morning, as I remember, it began as someone or ones tiptoed from room to room to make sure each sibling was awake so together we could go downstairs. The joy and excitement of opening gifts—always the "twisted ribbon candy" as it was known to us. Always there was the stubborn down drifting from the many geese we had picked and sold pre-Christmas. Yes, and now the dog is barking, and the doorknob rattles. It is the children from the four families to the northeast of us, and they have arrived with their skates and to show their most treasured gifts. We showed ours, quickly donned snow pants and warm jackets, picked up our skates, and went with them to the next few houses on the upper end of the island. Together, we took the woods road to the largest pond on the island. The lower-enders would join by way of the sea wall nearer to them in the morning.

As far as I can recall, all the preparations for Christmas Day were done on the twenty-fourth. As much as possible, firewood, water, and barn chores were done the day before, leaving Christmas Day free of work. Of course, there was the big meal of the day, and the headcheese and date-filled cookies that complimented the goose is still a delightful memory even yet.

When the day was almost over, we'd call over to Grandma and Grandpa, so they could come to the house for a visit. We would light the candles on the tree for a while. Then we would play the new games like Rook, Chinese Checkers, Crokinole, Flinch, Corneron, and Parcheesi, which had arrived under our tree.

All so long ago—almost a century has passed since those days on Inner Wood Island. They were marvelous Christmases, and it is my wish that this will be a marvelous Christmas for you, if not in fact, then let it be so in memory.

⋖ⓞⓞⓞⓞ⋗

The teller of this tale, a New Brunswicker living in Saint John, shared it with enthusiasm some twenty years ago, but upon seeing it in typescript, asked that it not be published while she was alive. As she has now passed on, the story is able to be told.

An Embarrassing Mistake, as told by Jean Taylor

My brother Russ reluctantly agreed to be Santa Claus for a Pentecostal Sunday school closing in the Clarendon area of New Brunswick. As it turned out the Pentecostal minister himself also wanted to be Santa Claus and had bought a suit for the occasion, but when he was told that Russ had agreed to do the job he demurred and attended the event with the scholars. The program consisted of recitations and readings and little playlets by the children. The highlight was to be the appearance of Santa. When it was getting close to the time that Santa Claus should arrive, he had not made an appearance. Not even the sound of his bells could be heard. The mistress of ceremonies—that was me—had listened hard. The minister was listening too and, unbeknownst to me, decided to take things into his own hands and went to get dressed in his Santa costume so the kids would not be disappointed. I later learned Russ had decided to stop for a visit at neighbour's home, had a couple of drinks, and had overstayed his visit. Upon realizing he was going to be late, he took off in great haste, hoping he wouldn't be too late arriving at the Sunday school hall. He was. The minister had dressed for the part, and when Santa needed to appear he had come in Ho, Ho, Ho-ing, and started to distribute the little trinkets and candy that had been arranged for the occasion. The mistress of events for the social—that's still myself—was pretty upset by the whole thing. In a quiet moment she walked over to Santa, who she—that's me again—thought was being played by Russ, and whispered in Santa's ear (that's the minister): "Russ, when I get you outside I'm going to kick your ass."

Now, I did not have any idea right then that I was talking to our minister, but I was soon to learn this, for what should happen but a second Santa Claus appeared at the back of the hall. Of course, it was Russ. The children were some surprised to see two Santas in that little schoolhouse, but not half as surprised—or embarrassed—as I was when I realized whose ear I had whispered those indelicate words into.

Oh yes, Russ got his just deserts!

⋖⟨⟨⟨⟨⟩⟩⟩⟩⟩⟩▸

Now a few of my own stories reflecting on my own early Christmas experiences, which were so meaningful that, as you've no doubt discerned by now, led to a lifetime love of the Christmas season.

The first story is self-explanatory and shares some of my dad's adventures as Santa, and some of my own!

Santa Abe and Son

My dad loved playing the role of Santa Claus in the fifties and he made a good one, being gregarious by nature and a whopping 240 pounds. My brothers and I always suspected it was Dad behind the beard when Santa showed up at school and church parties, but we were never certain. Then one year, we discovered his costume hiding at the top of a closet in the main entryway of our second-floor flat on St. James Street West.

"When Dad does his thing tonight," I told my brothers, "I am holding back to the last, and when I go up to him I am going to say, 'The jig's up, Dad, we know you're playing Santa.'"

So Dad came to me at the Sunday school party, as he always did, just before Santa was to arrive. He asked me to run the projector for the last reel of cartoons, as he had to leave. "Sure," I thought, "you're going to put the Santa suit on, that's why I got this job."

Well the movie ended, I shut off the machine. Dot Burpee played a few bars of "Jingle Bells" on the piano, and in bounced Santa. One by one, beginning with the youngest through to the elder students, the children went up, sat on Santa's knee, told him their wishes, and got a heaping bag of Ganong's chocolates, gumdrops, Chicken Bones, and hard mixture, which the teachers had bagged up the night before.

I waited until everyone had taken their turn, and then went up.

"Well, it's little Davey Goss!" Santa bellowed. "You've sure done a good job with that projector. Now sit down here and tell old Santa what he can bring you for Christmas."

I sat down, but did not say a thing about what I wanted. "Dad." I said, "The jig's up…fess up, there's no Santa, it's really you."

"Now, now David, you've got it all wrong. I'm not your Dad, I am really Santa. Why David, just look at the back of the hall, and who do you see standing there?"

It was my Dad! And he had a grin on his face that would have stretched across Carleton, as our area of west Saint John was known.

Well, Dad kept the mystery alive. Though in time, he did tell us that Mother had tipped him off after hearing us rustling in the shelf over the closet and discussing our plans, and that was practically the only time in our growing-up years that he got someone else to fill the Santa role for him.

Dad continued to play Santa for Kiwanis, for Cub groups, Sunday schools, and regular schools, but there was one time that he wasn't able to do it at church, and asked me to fill in. Now, I would never say no to Dad, but I should have. Being sixty pounds lighter than he was, even with three pillows I knew I could not fool those kids who knew me so well.

And I didn't. One of the little urchins lifted up my beard and announced incredulously, "It's David Goss playing Santa." One of the biggest daddies, Richard Burpee, rushed up to try to diffuse the unmasking, brushed the little one aside, and plopped his well-over-250-pounds onto my lap. "Now kids," he said, "Little Johnnie is wrong about Santa…and if you want your candy, you will have to come up and behave."

When the last of the kids had whispered in my ear and received his Ganong treats, the big daddy whispered, "Now that was a close call!"

Well, it was too close. Right then and there I decided that I would never play Santa again.

And I didn't for many years. Dad, however, continued to do so almost until his death in 2000. He loved to share stories of how entranced the kids were. One of his favourites was an occasion when he played the role for my sister's school in Quispamsis. It was one of those winters when there had been no snow, so, when asked how he was travelling, Santa told the kids he had a helicopter that year. In a great bit of serendipity, just as he left the school after doing his K-5 rounds, a medical emergency helicopter took off from a nearby playfield. My sister said there wasn't a disbeliever in the whole of the Quispamsis community after that.

Dad and I both sang with the Carleton Choristers, and a year or two before he died I conceived the idea that Santa should open up the concert by leading the Choristers into the church. Though his health was poor, Dad agreed to do it. At the last minute, he decided he couldn't, so it fell to me. It went fine, as I did not have to have any little ones sitting on my knee.

A few days later I was doing a writer's workshop, which always involved interviewing a guest. My guest could not come, so, as I still had the Santa suit, I donned it and had the participants interview Santa. Again, all went well…so well, that since I could do both these things again, and as Wal-Mart was clearing out Santa suits, I bought my own.

I have used it for many events since. I've told Santa's story dressed as Santa to seniors, been a special guest Santa at concerts, done storytelling as Santa, but not once have I sat and allowed children to whisper in my ear so I could pass them some candy. And I don't expect I ever will. As I said at the opening, I did not ever expect that I would play the role my dad did for all those years, but, as I have discovered in the several times I have done the Santa thing, there are some nice benefits. This was one of them.

I was leading a Walk 'n' Talk group in uptown Saint John. I was explaining how, in 1907, Walter Golding packed the Nickel Theatre when he arranged for the appearance of a live Santa. The success so impressed the Keith Albee folks in New York that they agreed to build the magnificent Imperial Theatre "in the sticks," which is what they called Saint John at the time.

To make the connection between the Nickel on Union Street (which is now torn down) and the Imperial on King Square South, I decided I should have a costumed Santa tell the story. I had Don Shaw in mind to do the job, as he does a great job in the malls of Saint John. But Don could not appear when the July night the Walk 'n' Talk was scheduled. So, I got my friend Harold Wright to talk to the participants in King's Square as I dashed ahead to the alley of the Imperial and donned my Santa suit. Harold was to lead the group over and I, as Santa, would share the Santa connection that continued at the Imperial until the 1930s.

I spotted Harold beginning to move the King's Square group toward me out of one eye, and out of the other, three teenage girls dashing toward me from Sydney Street. Their voices echoed in the alley as they screeched, "Oh! Oh! Oh! Oh, it's Santa Claus! It's Santa Claus! Oh! Oh! Oh!" I could tell they were excited to see Santa out of season. They rushed up to the alley, and without the slightest hesitation swooned in on me. The screams did not stop even as two posed on each side, while the other lifted her phone up and snapped a picture. "Oh! Oh! Oh! Hope you don't mind, Santa...our friends would never believe we saw Santa unless we showed them these pictures. We've been good girls, Santa, really we have!"

And a bonus for Santa, and the reason I will keep playing the role despite my intention to never do so, was as the young ladies finished, Santa's thank you was two teenagers kissing him affectionately on both cheeks!

⋘∘∘∘⋙

My mother was strict but fair. She expected a lot from her children and, as the oldest, I think she expected a lot more from me than she got. She had a firm rule about schoolwork. If you got an A or B, she signed her full name when you brought the test home. If you got less than that, all you got was MAG—her initials—to show that you had to do better to get her full approval. Here is one instance where I had to work real hard to win Mom over.

The Battle Over Mother's Mirror

When I saw Santa smiling from the windows of one of the bars at Market Square, it put a smile on my face too, and I didn't even have to go in for a drink! It reminded me of the mirror that hung over the mantle of my boyhood home on which I used to paint Santas each year when I was a teenager. I had quite a battle with my mother over it in 1957 when I proposed painting Santa on the outer panels, and a manger scene on the centre panel of the tri-panelled mirror.

Mother said, "NO! NO! NO!" the day I came home from New Albert School and announced that the students in my grade 7 class had just painted Christmas symbols on the windows of Mrs. Blenkhorn's home-room and I would like to do the same to our living room mirror.

Painting the school windows was a new idea to me at the time, as I had always attended La Tour School and had just gone over to New Albert the September previous. I got no support for the idea from my brothers, who were still at La Tour and had never seen the stained-glass effect the painting gave to the windows of my new school.

I was convinced in those days that I had artistic talent, and had already had a couple of my drawings chosen for the *New Albert Globe*, the school newspaper. So I expected my mother to be in support of the idea when I broached it.

She wasn't.

I knew no matter what I might say I could never wear her down just by nagging. But I tried anyway. As expected, she continued to say a firm NO! Dad didn't interfere. He knew better.

But I thought it was such a great idea, so I persisted. Finally, mother said, "How can you be sure that the paint will come off?"

"Well," I said, "I am sure Mrs. Blenkhorn would not let the windows be painted if it wouldn't."

"What kind of paint did they use?" she asked.

"Watercolours," I replied.

"Is that what you have?" she asked.

"Yes," I said. I was sure I had her in my camp by then. I was ready to get my paints and brushes out. But she fooled me.

"Ask Mrs. Blenkhorn tomorrow if she puts anything on the glass to make sure the paint will come off, and if she has ever tried painting on mirrors, and I'll see," Mother said, holding me up until at least the next day, for I was sure Mrs. Blenkhorn would answer both questions to Mother's satisfaction.

But she didn't.

Mrs. Blenkhorn said she put nothing on the windows that would assist the removal of the paint, and that she had never tried it on a mirror.

And I would not be allowed to either, Mother said with finality.

But I kept at her.

"David," she said after a couple more days of pestering her, "your track record around here hasn't been good this year. You got your broth-ers into trouble when you convinced them to paint the side of the house with mud. Then you broke off the lip of the concrete stairs pounding bricks into gold dust. Your uncle was mad enough about both those incidents. [He was our landlord.] Then you got his son in trouble when the both of you gathered up all the pumpkins in the neighbourhood and lit them on fire in the alley. Nearly burnt us out. You're likely to get a lump of coal in your stocking if one more thing goes wrong. So, we'll think about it next year."

Well, if you knew my mother like I knew her, you'd realize that her answer was final. NO! was NO! and would stay NO!

Imagine my surprise the following Wednesday morning when I came into the kitchen for breakfast and my paints were sitting on the table next to the bottle of milk, the Corn Flakes, and the stack of toast mother always had ready for her boys.

"What does this mean?" I asked.

"It means you can paint the mirrors," she said with a mother's smile that still radiates warmth to this day as I type these words.

"What changed your mind?" I asked.

"The ladies at church," she replied. I knew she had been to the Tuesday Evening Club the night before at St. George's, but I didn't see how they could have changed her mind when I had tried so hard.

Mother explained: "They had got to talking last night about how their kids were driving them nuts asking for this and that and the other thing. I got to thinking, 'David hasn't asked for one thing for Christmas except to paint my mirror,' so I am going to take a chance that the paint will come off."

Well, that afternoon I did the two Santas. As I recall it now, it was the next year before I added the manger scene in the center panel, because I really wasn't as sure the paint would come off as I had pretended to be. After all, I had not seen it come off at New Albert, and wouldn't until school resumed after the holiday.

So, it really was an act of faith for both of us that first year. When it came time to clean the mirror, it was easily done. Which was a good thing, for as my mother had said, I had enough black marks against me already that year to keep me off Santa's list for the rest of my life.

⋘⊙⊙⊙⊙⊙⋙

Mother was a top-notch cook, and her boys were top-notch snackers of her goodies. In the days when there wasn't always a nickel for a bottle of pop or a bag of chips at the store, there were always cookies in the cookie jar. But there was one type of cookie Mom could not make, even after Dad managed to get the recipe for her. Even though the cooking failed, we boys enjoyed it, as you'll see in this story.

My, Those Scotch Cake Crumbs Were Good

"Keep out of those sweets," my brothers and I would be told whenever Mother had made a batch of mocha squares, cherry balls, ginger jim-jams, or peanut butter cookies and set them on the kitchen counter to cool. When told that, we knew those sweets would soon be walked across west Saint John from our Blue Rock Hill home to our church, old St. George's. We also knew that we would not get to sample them, as they would be destined for adult mouths only.

Not that we didn't get cookies, we just didn't get the best cookies! Ginger snaps and sugar and vanilla cookies were usually in our cookie jar. With five of us dipping in, it was hard for Mother to keep that jar filled.

There were always more sweets on the counter and do-not-touch warnings in December than any other month, as there was a lot more going on at the church. Socials for vestry, Sunday school teachers, Wolf Cub leaders, and for Mom's Tuesday Evening ladies' club—where all the best cooking was taken.

One year Mom got the idea she would like to make Scotch cakes like our Aunt Dot did. Dot was famous for these buttery cookies, and everyone raved about them. She liked that and to keep it that way she refused to share the recipe.

Dot's husband was ill, so we boys and Dad did Dot's storm windows that year. As a thank you, she served us some of her famed cookies and Dad asked for the recipe.

"I don't share that recipe with anyone and even if I did, Marion would not be able to do them, Abie," she told him firmly.

"She's a great cook," Dad said pointing to his bulging belly.

"Yes, but you know it takes hours of kneading to do the Scotch cakes right, and with those kids of yours underfoot, well, Marion would just not have the time to do them right. All she would get would be a pile of crumbs."

Dad persisted and Dot gave in.

She was right. All Mother got was a pile of crumbs. But let me tell you—and I know my siblings would agree—they were some good crumbs!

It only happened once, though, for mother was a quick learner. Next Christmas we were all sent to board Dad's bus and go uptown to see the decorative lights as he completed his last bus trip of the day.

While we were away, mother kneaded and kneaded and later told us proudly the cookies were fine. Of course, at the time we had to take her word for it, as they all went to church! But in later years, we got enough of them to know she was right. None of them, however, tasted as good as that pile of crumbs did; our first taste of Mom's only-for-church cookies.

⌐ᘗᘗᘗᘗᕲ⌐

Here is the last of my memories of early Christmases in Saint John, which I wrote for the *Telegraph Journal* in 1981.

Reminiscences of a Christmas Tree

As soon as the Christmas tree is raised and decorated, there comes the inevitable comparison between the latest tree and those of the past. Somehow, the current tree never seems as big, or as bushy or bright and beautiful as the trees of former Christmases. Somehow, it seems to have a more crooked stalk, more gaps in the branches, more budworm damage, more burned-out lights, less ornamentation than the trees of Christmas long past. Only the passage of time will correct the deficiency list in any current tree, for the passing years seem to blur the memory of less-than-perfect trees of yesterday's Christmas.

Let me give you an example. Many years ago, we had one of those New Brunswick Decembers that began with a violent snowstorm. The fall had been deceivingly open and warm, and the Christmas feeling was found only in the minds and hearts of the merchants. But when the snow hit—*click!*—everyone began the ritual of shopping, crafting, practising choirs for Sunday school and school closings and thinking about getting their Christmas tree.

But the snow continued to fall and fall and even the tree vendors were having difficulty getting trees out of the snow-laden forest. City folks, many without cars in those times, watched anxiously as the price of trees skyrocketed—where there were trees to watch. Many lots were sold out, including those around our west Saint John home. Our family was getting concerned as Christmas approached and Dad kept saying we could celebrate Christmas perfectly well without a tree.

When the school holidays began and Monday and Tuesday had passed, and still a tree had not been brought into our house, my bothers and I decided to take action. At lunch we announced we would venture to Smuggler's Cove, some four miles down the Fundy Coast, where we had seen several fir trees while on a recent Scout hike, and would bring a tree home. We intended to walk, and Dad tried to reason with us, pointing out the difficulty of travelling in the heavy snow that had accumulated all month, and reminding us that wind-swept trees growing in salty environs of the Fundy shore are seldom suitable as Christmas trees.

But we weren't to be dissuaded, and insisted he leave the matter with us. As soon as he left for work, we struck out feeling quite proud to be able to carry out the task of procuring a tree.

As it turned out we never got to Smuggler's Cove. Just a few blocks from our home, a tree vendor had restocked his lot, and was selling some of the most pathetic trees one could imagine for the outrageous price of six dollars. We looked the trees over carefully, decided Dad was probably right about those on the Fundy coast, and while one brother remained as security with the tree we picked, two of us raced home, pooled our paper route profits, and went back to purchase the tree.

Having just parted with a week's earnings from our paper routes, we carried the tree home carefully, almost delicately. It couldn't have stood a rough journey anyway, being rather skimpy and showing the effects of three weeks of snow and a careless drag through the backwoods.

Once the tree was safely in our woodshed and the snow knocked off, it began to look a bit better, and we were anxious for Dad to arrive home and inspect our find.

It was well after six when he arrived, and to our chagrin, he was more interested in eating than viewing our tree. We would have none of that, though, and as he sat at the table, we opened the door from the kitchen to the woodshed, and snapped on the light so he could see the tree even as he ate.

We stood proudly between Dad and the tree, waiting for the pats on the back that we felt were sure to come. After a pensive moment or two, which seemed forever to us, he conceded that it wasn't a bad tree considering where we got it. We laughed, but we never told him the difference, happy to be thought of as gallant knights who had just fought and won the great challenge for their king.

After supper, at our insistence, Dad set up the tree, bracing it extra carefully lest a fall wipe out our treasure. He strung the lights, checked them out, and then disappeared. We finished the job and were glad to do so for we were anxious that the tree should be the most beautiful we had ever had. Thus, it got extra rope and tinsel, and every ornament we could lay our hands on, and twittering birds, and streamers, and candy canes, and lots of Christmas cards in the branches to hide the spindly spur. Finally, it was time to show the tree to the folks. They didn't get very excited about our effort. I don't know how they managed to contain themselves for we had created beauty where nature had failed.

Of course, with the passage of years I now realize that the whole thing might have been a well-planned plot on their part. They knew Christmas would come without a tree and tinsel, glass balls and streamers strung with icicles in our living room, and they knew in time we would come to realize that too, and perhaps it was time for us to begin the lesson. But that Christmas, we didn't know it, and it didn't seem possible there could be a Christmas without a tree. That fact motivated us to take the action we took and provided us with a Christmas and a Christmas tree we will never forget.

This final entry is not my words, but a selection of words by an unknown author who reflects my thinking after having put this book together. I hope you enjoy it and feel as I do about the many ways to celebrate the festive season.

An Old-Time Christmas on the Farm

From the *Family Herald and Weekly Star* of December 20, 1911. This account, written for a national audience, is abridged into sections to show the reader how little the Atlantic Christmas experience on the farm differed from that of the rest of county. As the country was very agrarian at the time of writing, it is truly reflective of what happened in the rural areas. But, as it is read, and from what has been presented in this book, it will soon be realized that it is also reflective or what was happening in many urban homes of the era, too. Thus, it seems a good conclusion to this work and is summarized here to show the many comparative points in the Christmases of yesteryear and those we celebrate now.

Where is Christmas Found?

"Oh, your true Christmas is found wherever he may be…on distant sea… with the lumberman in his camp…the bachelor settler in his shack…the miner in his shanty…in cities amid strangers…but wherever the wayfarer may be his thoughts will at once turn to the one spot which all the world holds most dear: home."

Preparing Food in the Old Farm Home

"How the memory likes to wander back to the old farm home and revel in the bustling scenes attendant on preparation for the Christmas festivities…when the poultry was sold and a couple of the best hen turkeys and several of the plumpest fowls did not go into the buyer's cart…great jars of mincemeat brought forth…cider applesauce is smelled simmering in a huge pan on the great range…the plum pudding compounded…the stuffing for the fowl prepared…the cakes mixed, the doughnuts rolled and cut into curious shapes, and the vegetables made ready."

Decorating Home and School

"As your memory wanders away again to the little district schoolhouse where as a boy you looked forward to the Christmas holidays—why did time lag?—Christmas seemed to dawdle in its coming. It was not because the boys and girls were idle...chief of all their tasks was that of providing the Christmas tree and evergreens for decorating the home, the schoolhouse, and perhaps the church. It required time to select the trees, collect fine boughs, haul them out to the winter wood road, and then, arranging the decorations...at the house, at the school...with the teacher as director. Diagonally across the ceiling festoons were hung and the black board, on which the school days hard tasks had been set forth, was now treated as an object of affection and framed with evergreens...and so, too were the windows and the doorway...and Christmas mottos were affixed to the walls."

Schoolhouse Christmas Eve Entertainment

"It was in the little old schoolhouse that the Christmas festivities often began with the School Christmas Tree being held on Christmas Eve. Never did scholars go to the old schoolhouse so cheerfully as on that night, and at no other time did the familiar room and the hard benches seem so attractive and comfortable. The parents went along with the scholars and the little place was crowded to overflowing. There was a chairman, usually a school trustee, and although he looked somewhat nervous he still cut a grand figure as he sat on the platform beside the teacher, or stood before them to deliver the opening speech.

The hero of the evening, however, was Santa Claus, the jingling bells of whose reindeer could be heard at the door although the reindeer never were seen. In came Santa Claus, always wearing a fur coat powdered with snow. Santa Claus, of course, wore a mask and flowing white beard, and after a little speech in which he recounted the perils of his journey, he proceeded to pluck the presents from the tree and to distribute them among the scholars. There were bags of candy and strings of popcorn, school prizes as the rewards of merit, and gifts and tokens of friendship and affection.

But this was only half the program—the other half was furnished by the scholars: recitations, readings, Christmas hymns, flights of oratory learned by heart from the dog-eared pages of readers."

Christmas Day In and Out of the Home

"In the dawn of grey light of morning you scampered down to see what Santa had done at home…the contents of the stocking were quickly examined, but the fruit of the Christmas tree was not plucked until later in the day. After breakfast the big three-seated sleigh was brought to the door to carry [us] to the village church. Never did a church service seem so long. […] Home again, and then came the Christmas dinner. After dinner the fruit of the Christmas tree was plucked and distributed. […] If the ice was good, there was skating, and coasting […] and in the evening neighbours came to chat with Father and Mother and sometimes the children noticed that in the conversation, there was now and then a note of sadness, and their elders looked backward and recalled friends that had gone with the Christmases of long ago."

Summing Up

"Time flies. Christmas may come and Christmas may go, and who should say that Christmas is not the better and the happier for the hallowed memories and associations of the 'old-home Christmas on the farm.'"

BIBLIOGRAPHY

꙰

The following texts provided invaluable background reading. Normally, these perusals led to research in various newspapers, which are always identified in the text. A collection of reference material from New Brunswick newspapers and other sources in respect to celebrating a Victorian Christmas were collected through the New Brunswick Historical Society, through an NB Labor Grant, January–March 1990.

A note on images: except where credited, all images are part of the author's collection and have been given to him or gathered from various sources.

Arsenault, Georges. *Acadian Legends, Folktales, and Songs from Prince Edward Island*. Charlottetown, PE: Acorn Press, 2002.

Bowler, Gerry. *The World Encyclopedia of Christmas*. Toronto, ON: McClelland and Stewart, 2000.

Croft, Clary. *Celebrate: The History and Folklore of Holidays in Nova Scotia*. Halifax, NS: Nimbus Publishing, 2002.

Del Re, Patricia and Gerard. *The Christmas Almanac*. New York, NY: Doubleday and Company, 1979.

Found, Emma. *To Love and To Cherish*. Hantsport, NS: Lancelot Press, 1977.

Glasner, Joyce. *Christmas in Atlantic Canada*. Canmore, AB: Altitude Publishing Canada, 2004.

Goss, David. *Old Tyme Christmas in New Brunswick.* Mount Pleasant, SC: Arcadia Publishing, 1997.

Grant, Francis W. *Courage Below and White Wings Above.* Hantsport, NS: Lancelot Publishing, 1979.

Hallett, Meghan, ed. *Diary of Sarah Clinch.* Halifax, NS: Nimbus Publishing, 2001.

Hamilton, William B. *Place Names of Atlantic Canada.* Toronto, ON: University of Toronto Press, 1996.

Jones, Ted and Anita. *Fredericton and Its People, 1825–1945.* Halifax, NS: Nimbus Publishing, 2002.

Marling, Karal Ann. *Merry Christmas.* Cambridge, MA: Harvard University Press, 2000.

Montgomery, L. M. *Anne of Ingleside.* Toronto, ON: McClelland and Stewart, 1939.

———. *Anne of Windy Poplars.* Toronto, ON: McClelland and Stewart, 1936.

———. *Anne's House of Dreams.* Toronto, ON: McClelland, Goodchild and Stewart, 1917.

Prince Edward Island Magazine. Charlottetown, PE: Archibald Irwin, 1899–1905.

Strom Collins, Carolyn, and Christina Wyss Eriksson. *The Anne of Green Gables Christmas Treasury.* Toronto, ON: Penguin, 1997.

Weale, David. *An Island Christmas Reader.* Charlottetown, PE: Acorn Press, 1994.

OTHER BOOKS by DAVID GOSS

Saint John West and Its Neighbours (1995)

Old Tyme Christmas in New Brunswick (1997)

150 Years of Caring: The Continuing History of Canada's Oldest Mental Health Facility (1998)

Saint John West: Book Two (1999)

A History of the Parish of Carleton : A Walking and Driving Guide to Saint John West (2000)

St. George and Its Neighbours with Elizabeth Toy (2002)

Brightening the Corner Where You Are: The History of Saint John Energy (2002)

Tall Tales and Curious Happenings (2002)

West Side Stories (2005)

History of Saint David's Church (2006)

It Happened in New Brunswick (2007)

Saint John Curiosities (2008)

Saint John 1877–1980 (2009)

East Saint John with Harold Wright (2011)

Only in New Brunswick (2011)

Historic Saint John Streets with Harold Wright (2013)

Saint John Ghosts (2014)

Saint John Snippets (2016)

Contributions in the Following Compilations:

The World Encyclopedia of Christmas (2000)

How to Have a Great Life (2006)

Christmas in the Maritimes (2006)

A Maritime Christmas (2008)

An Atlantic Canadian Christmas Reader (2010)

The Winter House (2011)

The Finest Tree and Other Christmas Stories from Atlantic Canada (2014)